THE
POTTER

KRISTY MARIE

First Line Editor: The Ryter's Proof
Second Line Editor: Fairest Reviews Editing Services
Proofing: All Encompassing Books
Cover Design: RBA Designs
Cover Photography: Wander Aguiar Photography
Formatting by: Champagne Book Design

For every woman who's ever struggled with imperfections.
You are beautifully magnificent.

THE
POTTER

Dear Reader,

In writing The Potter, I took massive creative liberties with, not only the law, but the field of medicine. Things that go down at Potter's Plastics do not generally happen in physicians' offices. You're welcome.

ENJOY!

CHAPTER ONE

Halle

Assholes come in all shapes and sizes.

This one, with his chestnut hair, pressed suit, and emerald green eyes, is the leader of them all.

"Serena!" he yells for the second time since I've been in his office.

"You better hope Serena comes in here with two of the burliest security officers you have," I threaten, nodding to the phone in his hand, "because I'm not moving from this chair unless someone drags me from it."

Dr. Potter, a world-renowned surgeon, and the man I traveled on a bus cross-country to see, tips his head toward the ceiling, and releases an exasperated breath. "That can be arranged."

I'll admit, most of Dr. Potter's frustration is my fault.

But had I known he was a giant asshole, I wouldn't have been caught off guard when he walked into this meeting, sporting a frown and the tightest ass I'd ever seen in a pair of slacks.

Not that I make it a habit of looking at my physicians' asses. But Dr. Potter, with his silent stare and snug pants, passed right by me, without so much as a hello, taking a seat in front of me and clipping out, "I can't help you."

He didn't even open my file. He simply turned me down in those first few seconds of meeting me.

I sort of… lost it.

Words were said and no apologies were made.

Until now, when he grabbed the phone and started dialing for security.

"Look," I jump up from my seat in front of the massive oak desk and put my hand over his. "I'm sorry. I didn't mean to be such an annoyance."

Dr. Potter allows the phone to click back into the cradle. A flicker of irritation crosses his face, and I take it as an opportunity to smooth things over and salvage this meeting. "Okay, I admit, I was pushy but not annoying." I hold his severe gaze, channeling all my pain and hope over the past four years into this one moment. "But you don't know how long I've waited for this meeting with you."

His hands travel to his suit collar, fingering the material. Could that be a sign he's cracking? "Understood, but like I told you twenty minutes and several insults ago, I can't help you."

This man… "I did not insult you."

He makes a scoff-like noise. "Asking me if I," he makes air quotes with his fingers, "'do layaway' is an insult to every surgeon I know."

"Who knew surgeons were so sensitive?" I slap my hand over my mouth. "I'm sorry. That came out wrong. All I meant was I didn't realize layaway was a big thing with surgeons. I assumed you all worked like a local K-Mart."

Dr. Potter doesn't find my humor funny as he rounds his desk, towering over me as his hands grip the armrest, caging me in.

Gah, he smells divine. Like leather banged a bottle of whiskey and spit out this devil with the face of an angel.

I struggle to find my voice with him this close. "I said I was sorry. Are you really going to hold that against me?"

The muscle in his jaw clenches almost rhythmically.

Don't reach up and touch it, Halle. I know it's been a long time since you found a man attractive, but this one isn't stable, and you've had enough psychos in one lifetime.

I stay silent, not even expelling a breath as I watch Dr. Potter work through the battle in his gorgeous head.

His decision is the key to my entire future.

Please say yes. Please say yes.

"Your comment is forgiven, but I still can't take on your case."

My heart drops back into the black void of my soul, where despair holds it.

"Now, if you'll excuse me, I have another appointment." Dr. Potter straightens, keeping his eyes fixed on me as he smooths his shirt, tucking it in like he isn't bothered in the slightest.

Honestly, I'm not proud of my behavior. I've waited years for this moment with Dr. Potter. He was the whole reason I endured hours of torturous physical therapy.

He was the light at the end of the tunnel.

And in twenty minutes, he snuffed out that flicker of hope.

My breath hitches as I inhale past the sob building in my throat. "You're my last hope. All the other surgeons I've consulted turned me down, too."

His entire demeanor changes as his body pulls taut. But I hold his gaze, conveying all the desperation and pain I've learned to live with for the past four years. "I need you. Please, just think about it. Give me time to earn the rest of the money you need to perform the surgery."

"It's not about the money," he clips, turning away.

Is he saying the surgery is too risky? "But you take risks. You heal the broken." At least that's what I've heard.

A tear slips down my cheek, just thinking about walking out of here without his help.

His heavy gaze tracks the tear as it falls to my chest. "I can't heal you, Halle." His gaze lifts as he pulls in a weighted breath. "I'm sorry."

Maybe it was the fact that I traveled eight hundred miles on a bus with no radio or the fact I was so excited for this appointment, I only got two hours of sleep. Whatever the case, the thread of sanity I had left, snaps. "You suck!"

I snatch the stack of cash tied together with a hair tie off his desk and stuff it back inside my purse. "You know what, Dr. Potter? You can go to hell. You're not the man the media said you were. You're a liar… just like every other man." I might be a little jaded in the men department.

The corner of his full mouth pulls up in a lazy tilt as if he's enjoying my meltdown in his office.

And it flips my freaking crazy switch. Again. "Fuuuuuuuck Yooooou!"

This time he does smile, softly chuckling as he takes me by the upper arm and guides me to the door, throwing it open and yelling, "Serena!"

I huff. "Sounds like Serena thinks you should go fuck yourself, too."

Warm breath coasts across my neck, tickling the sensitive spot under my ear. "Like you, Ms. Belle, Serena requires one thing from me—my skillful hands."

He shoves me forward, and I flip around to meet his eyes, swirling with emotion.

"I'll save you a seat in hell, Ms. Belle." He flashes me a wink that I'm embarrassed to admit sends tingles down low. "Right next to mine."

And then he closes the door in my face, effectively ending our appointment.

This mother—ahh!

I beat my fists on the back of his office door. My behavior is entirely unprofessional, but Dr. Potter's was unprofessional, too. How dare he insinuate that my actions are worthy of a fiery eternity. I came here to Texas for him. The newspaper promised he was different and wasn't like all the other surgeons I'd seen before. He would see through my past and change my future.

And he refused.

He was a coward, just like the rest of them.

All of this. Quitting my job, moving across the country, leaving my parents, my home, my entire life behind was all for nothing.

A sob bubbles up in my chest, but I swallow it down. I will not cry outside Dr. Potter's door. I will not give him another reason to think I'm unstable.

I'm not.

I'm hopeful.

And utterly devastated.

Inhaling, I situate my purse on my shoulder and stand up straight like a lady. My mother would be appalled that I used the F-word and insulted a world-renowned surgeon.

But she didn't see the way he looked at me as if our meeting was a complete waste of time after I had worked and saved for years, waiting eight months just to get on his calendar for a consultation.

I know what I'm asking him to do isn't critical. It won't save my life, but it has the potential to change it irrevocably.

I've earned something good, and he took it from me with one sentence. *I can't help you.* Of course, I was going to act crazy. This surgery has been all I've thought about for the past four years. I want it more than I've ever wanted anything.

More than a new car, a flashy career, or a home of my own. I want a fresh start—a blank canvas. And Dr. Potter, the fixer of broken things—the man who can mold a woman into perfection—was the only person who could give me back my dream.

And he said no. Not even that he'd think about it or consider it later when I had the full payment for the surgery insurance would not cover.

Just. No.

I hadn't expected a no.

I expected what the newspaper touted.

A brilliant surgeon.

A master sculptor.

Dr. Potter was supposed to take on the challenge and change my life like he's done for countless others, but he refused. Why? What makes my case so different than others I've heard about?

"Let me guess, he ordered a sandwich on rye, and you delivered wheat?"

My gaze whips to my left, and I find a grin with a head full of dark, messy hair. "Oh, I'm not a delivery girl."

His grin widens as he gives me a once-over. "I know, sweetheart. It just makes escorting you out of the building less awkward."

Ah. I nod. "You're security?" He certainly doesn't look like a Serena.

He motions to the hallway to my right. "Nope. Just a dutiful brother."

"Brother?" I give the dark-haired man another look. "You're Dr. Potter's brother?"

His mouth tightens. "Afraid so."

I wouldn't want to admit I was the rude-ass's brother, either.

I drag my feet as I follow him down the hall. "Did he ask you to remove me from the premises?"

"Ha. Vance would never *ask* me anything. Trust me, you don't want to be next to that door when he finally decides to come out."

"So, Dr. Potter does this often? Throwing women out of his office and all?"

A similar version of Dr. Potter looks down at me from his impressive height of likely six-foot. "Actually, I can't say that I've ever escorted one of Vance's patients out."

Great, so it's just me he hates. "I'm not his patient," I explain. "He refused me."

Like his brother, this kind stranger's dark brows pinch together. "Vance refused to treat you?"

I nod. "Yep."

Running a hand down his face, confusion lingers in his eyes. Clearly, that wasn't what he was expecting to hear. "Huh."

We round the corner and pass a desk full of women in various black pantsuits and skirts.

"Where's Serena?" my security escort asks the women.

"Lunch. Can we help you with something, Dr. Duke?"

I look up and watch as the charmer grins at the blonde. "Later. But call Serena now and tell her she's likely fired if she isn't in Dr. Potter's office in the next five minutes."

The blonde flinches and grabs the phone. "Certainly, sir."

A hand touches my back, nudging me forward. "See you later, Summer," he calls over his shoulder.

"Will he really fire Serena?" I ask, noting the exit sign and heading in that direction.

"Probably. My brother's mood has been a little volatile lately."

That makes sense. "So, you're saying I caught him at a bad time?"

Dr. Duke, as the woman called him, laughs behind me. "You caught him on a bad year."

"A year? He's been an ass—angry person for a year?"

That's not how his former patients described him at all.

"Yeah," he admits, a frown crossing his face. "It's been rough. I'm sorry you got caught up in his wrath."

I'm sorry, too. Had I known Dr. Potter's generosity was on a timer, I would have pulled more double shifts and made the trip to Texas sooner.

"That's okay." I sigh, staring at the ground as I follow behind him. "It was a long shot anyway."

Dr. Duke pauses at the door, his hand on the handle, hesitating. His mouth pulls tight as he stares at me with apologetic eyes. "I'd like to tell you to give him a couple of weeks and try again, but I'm afraid I would just be setting you up for more disappointment."

I swallow the emotion rising in my chest. "It's not your fault."

Dr. Duke opens the door. "It's not yours, either."

"Thank you for not really calling security when you heard me yelling."

That charming personality rears up again, as it had when we approached the desk of women earlier. "If anyone gets to escort beautiful women who piss off my brother out of this office, it's going to be me."

I can't help but let loose a genuine smile. "It was nice, sort-of, meeting you, Dr. Duke."

At least someone in this office was kind. The front-desk ladies were much like their employer—dry and soulless.

"It was nice meeting you, too, Ms...."

"Belle. Halle Belle."

The devilish charmer rubs his hand across his mouth. "Oh, Ms. Belle, with that southern name and accent... The trouble we could get into."

Clearly, Dr. Potter's office is lacking in the professionalism department, but I like that Dr. Duke made leaving less humiliating by offering me a compliment. It's been a while since I've heard one of those.

Duke being nice makes guilt settle in the pit of my stomach. I was mean to Dr. Potter. I'm not the woman who yells at a surgeon she respects. All I wanted was a chance, and Dr. Potter gave me one. His decision didn't go how I wanted, sure. But still, he gave me the chance I requested.

I just didn't realize how much hope I had riding on that one chance.

I flash Dr. Duke a sad smile. "Will you tell him I'm sorry for yelling?"

His grin fades, his shoulders dropping as his gaze briefly flashes to the ground. "I will. Take care of yourself, Halle."

Nodding, I gather my self-respect and walk down the hall toward the elevators.

And for the first time in four years, I have no plan, no direction, and no backup.

Dr. Potter took all of it with one inconsiderate slam of his office door.

CHAPTER TWO

Vance

"It smells like antidepressants and tears in here."

I lift my gaze from the file in my hand. "Did you end up calling security to escort Ms. Belle out?"

I raise a finger to the man sitting across from me, signaling for him to wait a moment while I speak with Duke.

"No," Duke chuckles. "She was quite sweet once I turned on the charm."

"The only thing sweet about that woman was her clothes." I stand and pour myself another drink, not giving a fuck it's during office hours. Ms. Belle was the only patient on my schedule today, and I knew last night when I reviewed her file, I wouldn't be taking her on as a patient.

"Come on, Vance, you and I both know the sweetest thing about her was *under* those clothes."

My hand tenses around the tumbler of bourbon. "Did you need something else, Duke?" I motion to the balding man in front of me. "As you can see, I'm busy."

"Nope. I just wanted to check on Richard here." He pushes the rest of the way into my office and shuts the door. "I'd hate for you to make him cry, too."

I can feel my earlier rage bubbling to the surface. Two glasses of bourbon aren't enough to get through this day. I need more, and I can't leave until I'm finished with Richard. "Continue," I bark out, ignoring the dumbass grin on Duke's face.

"As I was saying before," Richard clears his throat, awkwardly, "you asked me for my opinion, and I gave it to you."

"And as I was saying, I don't agree with your opinion, Dick."

The white-knuckled grip Richard has on his pen doesn't concern me.

"You don't need to *agree* with my opinion. But as your attorney, I suggest you heed my advice. Either you go to trial, or you'll be left to face the repercussions."

He taps the table, narrowing his eyes. "And you'll address me as Richard, not Dick."

I might appreciate the boldness if he wasn't tugging at his collar and sweating a river in my fucking chair. "Right now, your name is Fucking Fired, but Duke will take note of your preference for future meetings." I swirl the amber liquid in my glass. "Of course, you'll be wise to remember that I am to be addressed as Dr. Potter, not Vance or son."

Only Duke and Astor prefer weird monikers. Their patients refer to them as Dr. Astor and Dr. Duke which is completely unprofessional as surgeons.

"Everyone addresses me as Dr. Potter, Richard. And as my attorney, you will, too."

"Fine," Richard relents, shuffling the stack of papers in front of him. "Can we get back to the matter at hand? The lawsuit."

The mere word, lawsuit, has my eye twitching. Until now, I've never been sued in all my years as a practicing surgeon.

I run a hand through my hair, ignoring the shake in my hand. "As I said, I don't want to go to trial."

I can't face *her* again.

"But you did nothing wrong. Rolling over will set a precedence that this office won't fight frivolous cases."

The knot of tension coiled in my chest makes it hard to breathe. "I'm not sure the lawsuit is frivolous."

Richard sighs. "Dr. Potter, I know how you are with your patients, but this case isn't a burden you need to bear."

And Richard doesn't need to add to my already raging headache. "Are we done here?" I wave dismissively to Duke, whose expression has turned serious. "I need to get back to work." And to my drink.

Richard nods, exhaling a breath that irks me. "I'll set up another meeting with Serena for when you're more amenable."

Amenable is not in my DNA, but I offer him a curt nod anyway.

Whatever patience I had was used up when a cute blonde planted herself in one of my office chairs with her flowered-print skirt and wide blue eyes and refused to leave. I haven't been that amused since my brother dyed his hair blond for a woman going through cosmetology school.

But like Richard here, I snuffed the hope from her eyes, too. It's for her own good.

And mine.

As much as I would like to help Ms. Belle, I can't.

"The stakes are high, Dr. Potter. I advise that you get this mess behind you."

My gaze tracks back to the sleazy man in a designer suit, making his way to the door with less confidence than when he walked in here an hour ago. "I believe my name is on the outside of this door, Dick. I will put this 'mess' behind me when the mood fucking strikes me."

Unfortunately, Richard has some self-preservation and doesn't give me time to throw him out of my office like Ms. Belle did.

When the door clicks shut, I finally take a deep, soothing breath, but it doesn't last long.

"Five more minutes and Richard would have cried." Duke snaps his fingers. "It would have been a new record. Two in one day."

My gaze whips to Duke's. "I didn't mean to make Ms. Belle cry."

His brows arch. "Didn't you?"

"No." It's never my intention to make a woman cry. "But she wasn't taking no for an answer."

"Good women usually don't."

I scoff, reminiscing on Duke's many conquests, which never lasted past the third date. "What do you know about a good woman? You date women in seasons."

"At least I date. When was the last time *you've* been with a woman?"

It's been a long while, but I'd never admit it to my brother. He'd think it was a sin.

"Having sex with the employees violates policy," I remind him.

"Says the grouch who implemented such a travesty."

I take another sip of bourbon, enjoying the warmth coating my insides, drowning the demons. "We're never going to keep the front-office staff if you keep breaking their hearts, Duke."

"We don't keep staff because *you* scare them off."

What the utter fuck is wrong with the people in this office? "I haven't even been out of my office to scare anyone."

Duke shrugs, pouring himself a drink and taking a seat on the edge of the desk. "I don't mind giving the staff my undivided attention for satisfactory marks on this year's employee satisfaction survey, if that's what it takes."

"We don't administer employee satisfaction surveys," I add dryly.

"But we could. Think of all the things we could do to improve morale around here."

Morale will be the least of our worries if this lawsuit goes bad. But I don't mention that to Duke. The less he knows the better. "And I'd have eight lawsuits to deal with instead of one."

Standing, Duke turns serious. "What did Richard recommend you do?"

"He thinks I should take Calista to trial." A deep, heavy sigh claws out of my throat.

"Calista's been through enough."

"Agreed."

"So, what are you going to do?"

That is the dilemma. "I have no idea."

Duke seems to understand, taking another sip of bourbon. "Is that why you turned down Ms. Belle's case today?"

When you're a reconstructive plastic surgeon, you get used to seeing the worst cases, but sometimes the stakes are too high.… "Ms. Belle's case was too risky, not that it's any of your fucking business."

Duke arches a brow. "For you or her?"

And for the second time today, I throw another person out of my office.

"Don't be a pussy, Vance. Get up!"

I needed this.

After leaving the office early, I texted my older brother, Astor, who didn't bother coming into work, and asked if he was down for some sparring. I should have judged his mood more carefully since I'm the one on the mat, bleeding with his foot shoved in my back.

"I hear you like throwing women out of your office." He bears down harder, the burn of pain a welcome visitor.

Pushing up on my elbows, I gurgle out an unimpressive laugh. "And you call me a pussy?" I spit a mouthful of blood onto the mat. "I'm not the one gossiping with our little brother over salads."

"Duke is concerned. We both are." Astor steps off and kicks me in the ribs. Not enough to do any damage, but enough to serve as a warning. Out of the three of us, Astor and I don't do feelings. Concern is an emotion he'd rather bury right along with love.

I push up off the floor and stand. "I'm fine."

"She was your friend, Vance. It's natural to feel—"

I land a punch to Astor's jaw, bringing a smile to my face when he, too, spits out blood.

"All right, you little bitch. I see you're not in the mood to share. Enough talking for the day."

And we don't.

Instead, Astor and I trade blows for the next hour until I'm close to vomiting.

"Go home, brother."

I don't bother pulling my head from my hands and facing Astor. He can go fuck himself and his demands.

"I'm serious. Go home and get your shit together. Duke and I don't care how. Just as long as you get it done. If you don't start performing surgeries, we'll keep losing money. Winning the trial may be our only way to keep the practice open."

"Fuck you." I flip him off, still not moving my hands from my head.

My father founded Potter's Plastic Surgery. I offered to take it over when he retired, even though Astor was the oldest and next in line. But at the time, Astor didn't want the responsibility of running a practice, and Duke was still completing his fellowship.

I stepped up and took over the practice, rebranding and aligning my brothers' strengths with mine. The community needed a different image of plastic surgeons. We weren't vain and obsessed with perfectionism like my father.

We were constructors, sculptors, and refiners.

We built up the community. Healed the broken and gave hope to the hopeless.

And in four hours, I destroyed it all.

Ms. Belle wanted the old Dr. Potter—the one the media applauded.

What she got was the remnants of what that asshole left behind.

This Dr. Potter is nothing like that man she read about.

This one is sore, sick, and empty.

CHAPTER THREE

Halle

Actresses are good at being broke.

It's something you learn to live with in the entertainment business.

As for me, though, I've never been an actress or a starving artist. My ex took that dream from me long ago.

Now, I'm one step closer to living the life I've always wanted by renting a room in a shitty motel near the bus stop that probably should have been condemned a decade ago.

"The weekly rate is three hundred bucks." Clyde, as the sticker on his shirt says, slides over a brass key, completely ignoring the fishbowl in my hands.

I slap down some of the cash that I had tried giving Dr. Potter. "That won't be a problem."

I don't ask about the pet policy. If Clyde feels compelled to ignore Oscar, then I'm taking it as a green light that Oscar can stay. It's not like the motel has crystal wall sconces or a grand staircase leading to the elevator banks where the guests would be horrified by seeing a girl and her fish on the way up to her room.

Clyde's Motel is a one-level, L-shaped property, sitting off the main highway that leads into the city. What makes Clyde's charming, though, is the thin curtains and suspicious burn marks on the faded burgundy bedspreads. (The pictures on their website are of great quality.)

The point is, Clyde's has character.

"Your room is the last one on the right. We don't have breakfast or laundry services, so don't ask."

Clyde's blunt statement and immediate disappearance back into his office is amusing. I don't expect four-star customer service. I just need a place to stay while I figure out this whole Dr. Potter situation.

Grabbing my purse off the counter, Oscar and I head back outside, locating the last room at the end of the building.

It's a little sketchier than I thought it would be.

But I'm fine. I can handle a little dirt and danger.

"Let me guess, you're lost and bunking in this shithole for the night?"

The dark chuckle has me whipping my head around, finding a teenage boy who can't be any older than seventeen, lounging against the brick hotel. A cigarette hangs from his mouth, reminding me of one of those old cigarette cowboys.

"Should you be smoking?" I ask, tamping down my real question. What on earth is a teenager doing at a hotel that clearly is rented more by the hour than the week?

The boy flashes me a devilish grin. "You're definitely lost. You *and* your fish." He eyes Oscar like he's the stupidest thing he's ever seen.

"I'm not lost," I assure him. At least not in a geographical sense.

Personally, though? The FBI wouldn't be able to locate my sanity right now.

Ever since Dr. Potter dismissed me from his practice a week ago, I've sat alone in the hotel I rented until I could figure things out. Which hasn't gone so well. So far, the only thing I've figured out was that my checking account balance was dwindling by the day.

I couldn't keep staying in Texas with no job—surgery or no surgery. Either I go back home to my old life and admit that I failed in getting on Dr. Potter's schedule, or I stay in Texas and figure out what to do next.

The fact that I'm now moving into a hotel three times cheaper than the last one should tell you I'm not yet ready to admit defeat. I may not know what my next step is, but I know I'm not ready to give up a four-year dream just because Dr. Potter has been in a bad mood for 365 days.

"You need some help with your bags then?"

I eye the kid, who has now put out his cigarette on the wall, leaving a black smudge. "That's okay, I can manage."

He shrugs. "Suit yourself."

Tipping my chin, I grin, grabbing my bag from the ground. "I appreciate the offer, though."

"Sure."

Sure. It's not a get out of my office or a call to security. I guess I should be grateful. So far, my encounter with Texan men hasn't been all that great.

Hoisting the bag over my shoulder, I smother a groan from its weight and struggle to keep Oscar steady as I unlock the door. When it doesn't budge, I give it a shove with my hip, which is a terrible mistake as a zing of pain races up my side and sends me to the ground with a cry. In doing so, the bowl that housed my best friend smashes into pieces, leaving Oscar suffocating on the concrete.

The boy is in my face in an instant, an angry expression settling in his features. "What are you doing?"

I take a minute to regulate my breathing, pulling air in through my nose and out through my mouth, waiting for the pain to lessen. The pain isn't new, unfortunately. "I'm okay. Get my fish!" I wave my angry neighbor away, but it only makes him scoff while he scoops Oscar into his hand.

"What do you want me to do with it?" He closes his fingers into a fist, ensuring my little buddy doesn't flop back onto the ground.

"Put him in the sink or a cup—anything that will hold water," I beg. "Just, please, don't let him die."

He groans, probably because he can't believe he's saving a stranger's goldfish, and stands, throwing his shoulder into the door. Unlike when I did it, the door flies open, and I'm comforted by the sound of running water a few moments later.

"Looks like the fish will make it," he says, appearing in the doorway, his shirt dotted with water. He eyes me with concern. "How long are you here for?"

I scoot to the side and lean against the frame, making room for him to pass. "Don't know," I tell him, watching as he gathers the rest of my bags from the ground and sets them inside the door.

"You mean you're considering staying in this shithole longer than one night?" He shakes his head and chuckles, but it sounds more sarcastic than anything.

"Where are your parents?" I probe.

Turning, he heads into my room and strips off the sheets in one swoop, gathering them under his arm. "Where are *your* parents?" he finally replies.

I give him a flat look. "I'm serious. What are you doing out here alone?"

Those chestnut-tinted locks move with the shake of his head. "You don't belong here, but since I'm not in the mood to answer the cops' questions when you disappear, I'm going to help you."

"How generous," I mutter, and it makes him smile.

"I take Cash App and Venmo if you're feeling *really* generous later." He grins, and, in that moment, he looks every bit the teenager he is. "Can you get up?"

Testing the muscles, I stretch, only sensing the familiar ache I'm accustomed to. "Yeah, I think so."

He extends his hand, and I eye it warily. "You can take my hand, or you can struggle and fall again. Your choice."

This boy is going to be something else when he gets older.

"You're kind of bossy, you know?" Deciding that I could do worse than this teenager, I place my hand in his.

"And you're kind of stubborn." He pulls me up and holds on until I'm steady. "You good?"

I nod. "What are you doing with my sheets?"

"Not letting you sleep on them, that's for sure."

"What does that mean?"

He pulls the door closed with one hand and gives me the key. "It means we're going to the laundromat."

After stopping for supplies at my neighbor's room, where I didn't see any signs of a parent, my new friend and I walk two blocks to the laundromat, where we're currently waiting on my sheets and his shirt to dry.

"You never told me your name."

The teenager, who prefers sitting on an old dryer, looks up from the magazine in his hand. "Does it matter?"

"Yes, it matters." I try to mask my disappointment in his words. "I thought since you helped me—"

"Look, it's not a big deal. I help everyone."

His tense posture and constant frown make his statement a little hard to believe, but before I can tell him that, my phone rings. "I need to take this," I tell him.

He waves me off like he's relieved he doesn't have to speak to me any longer. I don't let it bother me. I know he has a mushy center underneath all the leather and frowns.

"Hey, Kristen," I answer, opting to forego the hello. Kristen doesn't care. She's been my agent and good friend for six years and works for the largest talent agency in California.

"Halle! I've got *big* news!" Kristen's eccentric squeals make me smile. "Maddox has a new movie coming at the end of next year. There are three available main roles. Auditions are in five months." She sucks in a breath and continues, "I talked to the bastard and told him you were finally getting surgery and would be ready for this next one!"

My stomach flips.

I might not be ready for this audition like she thinks. Not without Dr. Potter's help.

I also might not be ready to face Maddox again. The last time I encountered Maddox Keegan, a talented movie producer and grade A douche, I hadn't been out of the hospital long.

Maddox needed a fresh face for a new rom-com, and I was as fresh as they came, considering I'd yet to score an acting gig since college theater. The audition required a read in shorts and a bikini. Maddox took one look at me when I walked in with a cane and fresh scars and laughed, hollering, "Next!" before I even made it to the table.

That evening, Kristen broke the news that it would be harder now to land a job with my physical disabilities and scars, but there were parts I could play. We just needed to be patient.

It was the truth—the way of the world we lived in. You are judged on your looks before you even open your mouth. Maddox didn't need to see how amazing I could be in his starring role. He only saw the limp and scars.

He shattered my dreams just like my shitbag ex.

Everything I have ever wanted was gone in an instant.

But now, I'm here. Taking my life and my future into my own hands.

Fuck Maddox.

Fuck society and their loose morals and tainted codes.

I might not look like everyone else, but my will is stronger than theirs. I started out wanting this surgery because I needed to fit in with everyone else. But now, years later, I want this surgery, not because I need the scars to disappear, but to make the scars an exquisite reminder that there is beauty in every broken thing.

And broken things deserve a chance to shine just like everyone else.

"Halle? You there?"

I shake off the anger bubbling up. "Yeah, I'm still here. Tell Maddox thank you. I'll be there."

If only to flip him off.

"I can't wait to see you! I'm so jealous Dr. Potter is making you even more stunning."

Not exactly.

I might have withheld the information from Kristen that Dr. Potter turned me down. She was so excited and worked so hard getting auditions for me so I could immediately jump back into the business I'd longed for. I couldn't let her down by telling her I offended Dr. Potter and was thrown out of his office.

"Yeah, I can't wait for the new me," I lie, waving off my neighbor's scowl and walking out of earshot. "Dr. Potter's schedule is tight, though, but he assures me he can see me tomorrow." I hold back a guilty sigh as I lie once more.

"That's great to hear. I'm rooting for you, Halle."

"I'll call you as soon as I see Dr. Potter."

I can hear Kristen's perfectly-manicured hands clapping together from excitement. "Great! We'll figure out all the details after you recover. This is your time, Halle! Talk soon."

It's my time.

Mine.

Kristen is right.

No one, not even Dr. Potter, will take my dreams away from me again.

I hang up with renewed energy and some sense of a plan and find a grumpy teenager eyeing me while folding a dingy sheet. "You're pretty good at lying," he notes.

"And you're pretty good at folding. Who taught you how to fold a fitted sheet like that?"

He rolls his eyes as I approach. "I moonlight at the dry cleaners during the summer."

I grin. "Now who's lying?"

Grabbing the other sheet, I start folding with ideas of how to get back on Dr. Potter's schedule racing through my head.

"Are you sick?"

Raising my eyes slowly, I meet the gaze of the nicest person I've met during this trip, even if he won't tell me his name. "Not anymore."

"Then why do you need to see this Dr. Potter guy?"

I grin. "How much is the information worth to you?"

The boy is immediately on alert, his body coiling tight before my eyes. "It's not worth anything. I was just making small talk."

Lies. This little hero in the making is actually concerned about me. Shrugging, I offer him a playful grin. "Tell me your name, and I'll tell you what business I have with Dr. Potter."

He's quick to respond. "No."

"Suit yourself." Foregoing the rest of the folding, I wrap my arms around the clean sheets and blankets. "Thanks for the help, neighbor. See you around."

His glare tracks me as I bump the glass doors with my hip and head back to the motel, where I finish putting on the sheets and making a list of everything I think I can fit into the mini fridge. Staying here and waiting for Dr. Potter's mood to improve will require money, and that's something that's currently dwindling as each day passes.

First order of business is groceries, and the second is a job.

And third, is planning Operation Beg Dr. Potter for a Second Chance.

CHAPTER FOUR

Halle

"When you're finished scanning all the groceries, you hit this tender button right here and give them the total."

I found a job.

It's minimum wage and requires me to be on my feet eight hours a day, enduring training from a five-year-old. Okay, she's more like sixteen, but still, I never thought, at twenty-three years old, I would be working at the local supermarket with a supervisor who just got her driver's license.

"You think you got it?"

I flash the sweet, gum-chewing girl a smile. "I think I can manage."

She bounces on the balls of her feet. "Okay, cool. If you need me, just holler. I'll be over there, helping Evan stock produce."

With one quick look at Evan, I can tell you the only thing he'll be stocking is his supply of condoms for tonight.

"No problem. Thanks for the help, Brit."

Apparently, Bloomfield, Texas, home of the famous Dr. Potter, isn't short on vacant job openings. My neighbor, who still won't give me his name, caught me with a newspaper out on my front deck a few days ago. And by front deck, I mean front stoop, where he likes to smoke and leave his butts on the ground. He suggested I come here to Whole Grains and ask for Sammy. I didn't ask how he knew Sammy or who Sammy was. I desperately needed a job if I wanted to stay in my not-so-lavish motel room while I figured out a way to get on Dr. Potter's good side.

A girl can't be picky when she's desperate. And I've never been more desperate to fulfill my goal of being one of Dr. Potter's patients.

"Hi. Welcome to Whole Grains!" I chirp to the man who saunters through my line, his phone pressed to his ear.

He tips his chin at me, and mouths *hello* as I begin unloading and scanning the groceries in his basket.

I'm halfway through his items when he ends the call and pockets his phone, flashing me a charming smile that seems familiar. "You new here?"

"Yeah," I nod, trying not to stare at the outline of muscles he has crammed into that white button-down. "I just started a couple of days ago."

"Next time, you're going back for the fucking wine. What man drinks wine, anyway?"

A bottle of pinot slams down on the counter just as the voice that sounds eerily familiar, too, adds, "Well, look what we have here." Dr. Duke, grinning wider than a football field, slaps the man's chest with the back of his hand, making me edgy. "This is the girl I was telling you about."

The guy, who has muscles for days, arches his brow, immediately perking up. "The one that made Vance cry?"

"That's the one!"

"I did not make him cry!" I nearly shout. "You are severely exaggerating the story." Pointing an accusing finger at Dr. Duke, I address the new guy. "He's lying. I didn't make Dr. Potter cry. I swear. I was just having a bad day and well, Dr. Potter was…"

"An asshole?" the new guy suggests.

"A glorified dick?" That was Dr. Duke.

Sighing, I pick up another item and scan it, just so I don't have to look them in their eyes. "Dr. Potter disappointed me is all."

Dr. Duke scoffs, popping the other guy in the chest again. "Told you. He wouldn't take her on as a patient. Since when have you seen him do that?"

The man's eyes narrow. "Why did he turn you down, if you don't mind me asking?"

I really don't want to rehash my conversation with Dr. Potter, but perhaps Dr. Duke and this new guy will have some pull and convince the good doctor to see me again. It's worth a shot.

"I'm five grand short for the procedure I need, but Dr. Potter said even if I had the money, he couldn't help me." I point to the groceries in front of me. "I know money talks, so I figured I'd save up and see if that changes his mind."

"He won't change his mind."

My hand pauses as the new guy crushes my soul once again.

"Not for money anyway," he adds.

Burying my emotions way, way down, I keep my head low and nod, getting back to their groceries.

"I'm just saying, Vance has money. You won't get anywhere taking that angle."

The way he says this is almost like he's leading into giving me some advice, and I'm all for helpful hints when it comes to my future and Dr. Potter.

"What angle are you suggesting?"

The new guy reaches into his pocket and hands over a card.

I look at it and then look again.

"Dr. Astor Potter." You've got to be shitting me. "Let me guess, you're another brother?"

He grins, and I realize the familiarity is because Dr. Duke smiles exactly the same. "The oldest. And I've recently found myself in need of a secretary." Annoyance lingers in his eyes as he glares at Duke. "Someone ran my last one off with a break-up text."

Duke shrugs, completely ignoring his brother's hateful look. "She's the one who wanted more. She knew the deal. One season only."

Dr. Potter or Dr. Astor, whatever he prefers to be called, shakes his head. "Anyway, if you can answer the phone and incite rage in my brother, like you did the other day, then you're hired."

What? "I don't understand."

The eldest Potter leans in over the register, close enough I can smell his woodsy cologne. "You want on my brother's operating schedule?"

I nod.

"Then don't take his no for an answer."

I don't know if it's the smell and the all-around vibe of the Potter brothers, but I stay frozen as he chuckles. "Tell Sammy I'm sorry for stealing you and then meet me at the office tomorrow at nine."

Am I really considering this? A job at Potter's Plastics?

It does get me closer to Dr. Potter and allows me the time to change his mind or spike his coffee with something that puts him in a better mood.

I find myself nodding in an instant, agreeing to meet Astor tomorrow morning.

Astor shoves cash across the register. I don't even remember giving him the total. "Keep the rest. I'll see you tomorrow. Don't be late." He flashes me a wink. "That's my thing."

That night, as I tried to get comfortable, all I could see was Dr. Duke's smirk and Dr. Astor's fist bump as they chuckled all the way out the door.

Whatever gift I'd just been given, I would soon learn it was merely a nightmare wrapped up in pretty pink hope.

"Leave before I call security. I don't have time to deal with this today."

My mother would call this woman a witch, but I'm not my mother, and I think she deserves a far uglier word. One that rhymes with twat-inator.

"I'm telling you, Dr. Astor—or Potter—told me to meet him here this morning." It's only the fourth time I've said this, but based on the blatant disbelief, I'm going to need to say it a few more times and call Dr. Astor so he can confirm it.

The redhead with the pantsuit and attitude turns to her coworker. "Call Dr. Potter. He's the only one here right now. He'll know if Dr. Astor hired a new secretary."

Oh, no. No. No. No. No. "It was a last-minute thing. I doubt Dr. Potter knows anything about it."

"Dr. Potter knows everything. Don't worry, we'll get this sorted out."

I hate patronizing bitches.

"Dr. Potter, the patient you dismissed last week is at the front desk, claiming she's Dr. Astor's new secretary. Would you like me to call security?"

I don't need to hear what he said, the I-told-you-so smirk on her face is evidence enough.

"Sure. I'll make sure she stays put."

Great, just freaking great. I knew it! I knew this was a bad idea, but again, I'm desperate, and Dr. Astor and Duke seem like fun guys. Why can't their brother be cool, too?

"Dr. Potter will be with you in a moment."

I almost flip her off. If I'm going to be thrown out of this office twice, I'm not going out with manners this time. Well, I didn't last time, either, but I tried to make it right in the end.

"Ms. Belle." Dr. Potter's smooth baritone guides my head up on its own accord.

Why? Why must he look like he just rolled out of bed and threw on an expensive suit? Why can't he look creepy or be old? Anything to make him less attractive. It was like God knew women would want to murder him with that rude-ass attitude, therefore he made him hot, so we'd at least not stab him at the first meeting.

"I thought I made myself clear last time. I can't—"

"There she is!" Relief settles in my stomach as Astor's familiar voice drowns out whatever lecture Vance was about to give me. "Sorry, I'm late, darling."

Astor throws his arm over my shoulder. "Come, let me show you to your office." He pulls me beside him and through the half door separating the waiting room from the staff. I can't help but smile as Red's mouth drops open in shock. *Suck on that, Miss Thang.*

As we pass by the desk, Astor pauses. "Vance. Glad to see you're sober and a little less murdery this morning."

Dr. Potter's jaw tightens, and I really hope Astor's plan wasn't to piss him off this early. I really would like us to be on civil terms if I ever hope to be his patient.

"Astor," Vance grits, faking a tight smile. "Glad to see you could make it in today. Perhaps we should have a meeting. I seem to be behind on a few changes around the office."

Astor chuckles and starts moving us forward. "Agreed. See my secretary and she'll set something up."

Without giving Vance time to argue, Astor pulls us down the hall and past Duke's office, where he has a blonde cornered against his desk. "Your office is next to mine at the end of this hall. I don't care what you wear, just as long as it isn't a black pantsuit."

I hesitate. "But doesn't the rest of the staff wear black?"

Astor stops in front of an oak door—just like the one I beat on when Dr. Potter pushed me out of his office—turning with a shit-eating grin. "Vance likes order and black."

The wink he gives me is clear. *Stir up some shit.*

"I like pastels," I add, my voice unsure if my intuition is right about what Astor's objective is.

"Pastels just became my new favorite color for work attire." The confidence in his voice makes me smile. Maybe working here won't be so bad after all.

Astor pushes open the door to my new office and reveals a wide, expansive desk, gleaming in sunlight from the floor-to-ceiling windows behind it. "I've never worked somewhere so beautiful," I admit softly.

"A beautiful office for a beautiful lady."

With a small nudge, Astor ushers us into the space and points to the door to the right. "I'm just through there. Familiarize yourself with the office while I return a couple of calls and then we can go over the basics."

I nod, watching as he unlocks the adjoining door. "Dr. Astor?"

He turns around, his voice full of curiosity. "Yeah?"

"Thank you for the job."

"Don't thank me yet, kid."

CHAPTER FIVE

Vance

"Was this your idea?"

There weren't enough deep breaths and stress squeezes to calm me down after seeing Astor and Ms. Belle who, apparently, now works here.

"Why would you think I had anything to do with this?" Duke kisses Carmen—not *Summer* as he calls her—on the cheek and swats her butt, ushering her out of his office and back to work, where she should have been half an hour ago, instead of making out with my brother.

"Because," I snap, "you were the only one who knew what happened between me and Ms. Belle." Astor wasn't here the day I threw Halle out of my office. Clearly, Duke told him, but he wouldn't have known where to find her or even know what she looked like. This could have only been Duke's doing.

He throws his hands up, laughter making his whole body shake. "I might be going through a dry spell right now, but trust me, the last thing I want to do with my time is come up with ways to piss you off."

I disagree. He and Astor love to add chaos to my order. "She shouldn't be here," I grit. "We have no idea if she's crazy or only using this job to get what she wants."

"And by what she wants, you mean a surgeon who can help her?"

A rush of shame coats me from the inside.

"You have no idea what her history is," I argue.

Duke walks around to his desk and sits. "You're right, I don't. Show me her chart. Maybe I can help her."

"No."

My hands tremble as I remember the images of the scars on her hip and thighs.

"No? You won't show me? Or no, I can't help her?"

Why is he pushing the issue? "No to both. Neither of us can help Ms. Belle. She's not here for tits; otherwise, I would have sent you the case last week."

Total lie. Even then, I wouldn't allow my brother to take my patient.

Duke chuckles. "I might not be as good as you are with scars, but I likely could make them better than what she currently has."

"No."

I don't even know why he's challenging my decision. Never have my brothers butted into my treatment of patients.

"Fine," he chuckles, "but don't be surprised if Astor offers her a consult." Shrugging, he boots up his computer like he's done with the conversation. "She seems like a really sweet woman. I don't see the problem."

"The problem is..."

He lifts his head, waiting, and I stop. I don't owe these fuckers an explanation. My patient, my decision. "Never mind. I'll take up my issues of her current employment with Astor."

"You do that." He smirks.

I turn from the office without another word.

Fuck Duke. Fuck Astor. Fuck this whole fucking practice.

"Dr. Potter!"

I suck in a deep breath before turning around. "Yes? What is it,

Serena?" Did I not just tell her everything she needed to know five minutes ago? What could she possibly need now?

"Um, your nine thirty is waiting in exam room one."

Fuck.

"Fine, I'll be there in just a moment."

Right after I speak with Ms. Belle and fucking Astor.

Without turning back, I continue down the hall toward Astor's office and pause at the only open door. Halle's.

I expected Astor wouldn't want to deal with me and lock his office door, forcing me to go through Halle.

Fine.

It's not like Halle will be my problem if things go bad.

"Ms. Belle," I state, striding in and catching her sorting through one of the desk drawers. "I need Astor's first available appointment this morning."

Her head darts up, and she stands, smoothing her black and white houndstooth dress just like she did the last time I saw her. "Hi."

I don't bother with the niceties. "His first available. Let Serena know the time." I turn and take a few steps before adding, "And the dress code is all black. No patterns."

I'm at the door when she retorts, "Good thing I don't work for you."

Turning slowly, I face our newest employee. "I'm sorry, what?"

She stands straighter, her face taut and firm. "I said, good thing I don't work for you. *My boss* encourages variety."

Fury radiates in my bones, and I find myself taking an unconscious step closer. "Does he now?"

She takes a step back. "Yes, when Astor makes time for you today, you can discuss my dress code with him. Otherwise, have a great day, Dr. Potter."

I nearly cut off the circulation in my hands clenching them so tight.

"Is there anything else you need?"

Her shaky tone pulls me out of the fog of rage.

What the hell am I doing?

I take a step back, releasing a breath. "Give Serena a time."

With that, I get the fuck out of her office before I lose my shit and embarrass myself further. Clearly, something about this woman brings out the beast in me. Honestly, she hasn't done anything but call me on my attitude. But still. No one, and I mean *no one*, calls me on my attitude.

Who does she think she is?

It doesn't matter. She's Astor's problem. He hired her, and he'll deal with the aftermath of her temper.

"Serena!"

The redhead who's been my secretary for the last five years appears. "Yes, Dr. Potter?"

"What room again?"

Dealing with Ms. Belle has made me crazy. I would have never forgotten a room number in a matter of minutes.

"Room one, sir."

I nod, noting how put together she looks with her sleek black pantsuit. Not at all like Ms. Belle with her ruffled houndstooth and messy hair thrown together in a braid over her shoulder.

"I'll send in a nurse," Serena adds as I turn around, already striding toward the hall where my first patient of the day awaits. Seeing patients now is a torture I never thought I would experience. Burnout tends to happen to surgeons after years of practice.

Losing patients, bad outcomes, and hopelessness will inevitably take its toll, but I never thought it would happen to me, not this early in my career.

But it wasn't several patients and multiple outcomes that sent me spiraling into who I am today. It was one patient, one bad outcome that ruined my devotion to the craft. It triggered a wave of insecurity that I've never dealt with.

I am *the* Dr. Potter.

I perfected the imperfections that haunted my patients.

I gave them hope. Peace. And a fresh start.

And with one mistake, with one patient, I took the hope from all of them. Just ask Ms. Belle.

Standing outside room one, I take the folder from the plastic holder on the wall and scan it.

Carly Sims, a thirty-four-year-old single mother of two. She suffered third-degree burns to the left side of her face and body while shielding her son from flames as they escaped a small house fire. The boy suffered superficial burns that healed without treatment. She wasn't so lucky.

She saved her son, and now, she needs me to save her.

A knot forms deep in my stomach as a wave of nausea sweeps over my body. I don't want to enter this room and give the woman hope when I know I can't deliver on my promises.

Like Ms. Belle, Ms. Sims has been on my schedule for months. Before I realized I couldn't operate anymore. If I'm honest with myself, it wasn't the lawsuit that changed things.

It was *him*.

It was looking her in the eyes, smiling and hopeful that I fixed an imperfection that plagued her husband. It was holding her in my arms as she beat her fists into my chest, wailing that I was a liar. It was when she finally tired and crumbled to the floor, her body curling into itself as she blamed me. Hated me.

It was the first time I'd failed.

The first time I had disappointed anyone.

It was the first time I lost a patient.

And it killed every bit of good inside me.

I was no longer a savior, but a killer.

And I'm stuck, hiding behind the monster and giving people like Ms. Sims false hope.

"Dr. Potter?" Autumn—her real name, not a nickname from Duke—pulls me from my thoughts. "You ready?"

I nod, giving the solid wood door a frown.

Just fake it. That's all you need to do. Give Ms. Sims the hope and solutions she deserves.

"Yeah, I'm ready."

Twisting the handle, I open the door and force out a smile at the woman sitting atop the table. "Ms. Sims," I greet her, extending my hand. "It's a pleasure to meet you."

The skin on her cheeks reddens, darkening the rigid flesh there. "You're um…" She shakes her head. "I mean, it's very nice to meet you, too. I've been looking forward to this appointment for a long time."

Unfortunately, she's not the only one.

The knot in my stomach tightens, strangling me from the inside out.

"So, tell me," I try for a change of subject, "how you've been since," I glance at her chart, "the infection."

Like with most burns, infections are common. In Ms. Sims's case, she had consistent bouts of them, requiring debridement of her wounds and many painful surgeries. She's had several months now being infection-free, which is why she's here.

"I've been great." Her face brightens as she begins to fill me in on all her accomplishments amidst the infections and setbacks she's had this year. "I can't wait to get back to the old me!"

But that's just the thing, I can never give them back what they had.

The "old them" is gone in the same way that the old me is, too.

I take a step closer, taking her hand. "I can't promise the old you, but I can promise a new you."

Ms. Sims's chin quivers, and I know she's letting that blow sink in. Back to the time when she was scar-free—when the only worry was a rogue gray hair and fine lines. Tears well in her eyes as she fights them off, squeezing my hand tightly. "Anything is better than seeing my son cry when I show up at school." She tries shaking off the memories I've heard from so many others. "Kids are so cruel…"

Adults are, too, but like most moms, Carly worries more about how her looks affect her child's life. It's a painful reminder of why I chose reconstruction as my specialty.

And why I can't do it any longer.

I squeeze her hand. "Save your tears for recovery."

Her strength literally forms in front of me as she straightens, talking as I examine the worst of the burns, noting in her chart where I can take the skin from and where I can tighten to reduce the look of the burns.

It's something I couldn't offer Halle.

It's something I can't offer Ms. Sims, either. Not yet anyway. All I can do is put her on my schedule and hope I can pull myself together before her surgery date.

I leave the room with a forced smile before I make it to the bathroom and retch.

Who the fuck am I kidding?

I'll cancel on Ms. Sims, just like I canceled all the others.

I can't operate on them.

I can't take that chance again.

I can't be a killer.

Getting up, I lean back against the wall next to the sink and slump down to the floor as my chest tightens and my breathing turns shallow.

No, no. Not now. Not at work.

Focusing on my breaths, I put my hand to my wrist and try to slow my rapid breathing, but it's no use. This feeling is one I've become very acquainted with lately, therefore I know when I've lost control, and I let the darkness consume me.

CHAPTER
SIX

Halle

I waited too long.

Really, I shouldn't have taken the extra cup of coffee Astor offered me. But I did, and now, I'm wandering around the endless halls searching for a bathroom.

I could have asked Serena, but my gut said she would ignore me, and I hit the quota of dealing with twats today. Besides, how hard could it be to find a bathroom? Generally, they are labeled. Which was how I finally found one, two halls over from my office.

A simple oak door with a gold plate labeled *Restroom*.

Not *Women's Restroom* or *Men's Restroom*. Just *Restroom*.

So, I pushed it open, already pulling at the bottom of my dress before coming to a halt.

Slumped on the floor, a dark head is bowed over his legs. "Dr. Potter?"

Now, if this were any other person, I would have rushed to his side, but this is the man who threw me out of his office and looks at me like I'm the very last person he ever wants to see again.

So, I hesitate.

It's a natural reaction.

You wouldn't run headfirst into a lion's den, would you?

No. Exactly. I don't have a death wish.

So, I try again. This time louder. "Dr. Potter, are you alright?"

I mean, maybe he's such a day drinker that he catches naps on the bathroom floor? I, personally, love to nap in a hammock, but to each his own.

Dr. Potter doesn't answer me, so I bravely creep closer, stretching my hand out carefully. "Vance?" I truly expected a reaction after addressing him by his first name. "Can you hear me?"

I can see his chest rising, so he's definitely breathing. That's a plus. The last thing I need is to call the coroner to take away the only man who can help me.

That would be some terribly shitty irony.

Placing my hand on Vance's shoulder, I squeeze, giving it a small shake, and wait.

And wait.

Great, my future surgeon is a drug addict. Seriously, if he's OD'd, I'm going to be seriously disappointed. But I would accept his decision. Eventually.

Standing, I go to the sink and wet the fancy hand towel hanging from a gold hook. I give it a few twists and say a small prayer that Vance doesn't scream at me when he's finally conscious.

Lifting his head gently, I can't help but notice the lines in his face, pinched, like even in his unconsciousness, he's not content.

My chest tightens, forming a band of pressure around my heart.

We all have demons, don't we, Dr. Potter?

I brush the damp, chocolate curls from his face, taking a moment to admire the pouty frown and sharp cheekbones. If his eyes were open, I would admire the dark lashes framing a brilliant pair of emerald green eyes.

Dr. Potter is living, breathing art. Beautiful beyond what is fair.

"Vance," I whisper carefully, pressing the cold towel to his forehead. "Open your eyes."

With one last shake to his shoulder, Vance's eyes flash open, going from confused to angry in a matter of two slow blinks.

"Get away from me," he growls, snatching the towel from my hand and tossing it.

"Oh, you're welcome." I ignore his ungrateful comment. "I was just about to wet my pants, but I saw a demon on the floor and thought, *might as well help the jerk of the world before I take care of my own needs.*"

He draws his knees up. "What are you doing in my bathroom?"

"This is *your* bathroom?" I look around, trying to find any indication this is a *Vance Only* restroom, and find nothing. "I didn't see a sign."

He narrows his eyes like I'm the dumbest person he's ever seen. "It's on my hall."

I stand, putting much-needed space between me and the grouchy surgeon. "My bad. Astor hasn't finished telling me what halls I can use." Eyeing the toilet behind us, I add, "But while I'm here…"

Vance stands and shoots me a look over his shoulder as he turns on the water, washing his hands and splashing water on his face. He looks so broken in that moment that I can't help myself. "Are you okay? Do you need me to get one of your brothers?" I mean, he was really out of it.

"I'm fine."

I meet his hateful gaze in the mirror. "Are you?"

It was the wrong thing to say. Vance whips around and eats up the space between us with big strides, forcing my back against the wall. "Don't let your research fool you, Ms. Belle. I'm not the savior you think I am."

His eyes roam my face heatedly.

"What are you then?"

Dr. Potter swallows harshly, his hands going to my arms, gently squeezing. "You don't want me to save you, Peach. You want to run and never look back."

With that, he releases me and is gone before I can even take a breath.

I stand, rooted in place for I don't know how long, my arms still tingling with his touch.

Dr. Potter is… intense. Dramatic. And likely a bit pessimistic. But whatever happened to him last year to cause this mood, it isn't who he is. Trust me, I've been there. I've been in his shoes.

Tragedy changed me, killed a part of me. It took a long time for me to come around and realize that the woman I was still lived in this different body. She was different, sure, but she was still there. It was only a matter of coaxing her out.

I choose to believe Astor and Duke. Something happened to their brother that really affected him. Like me, he just needs a goal and time. The old Dr. Potter will return eventually.

At least, I hope.

By the time lunch rolled around, Astor had given me the rest of the tour—never mentioning the banned hallway that is Vance's—showing me how to work his calendar and the labeling of his patient files.

He also assured me the staff, who I've now started calling the Pantsuit Brigade, will warm up eventually.

Again, I don't take their scrutiny personally, only one of them had a wedding band on their finger, and I'm sure landing one of the Potter surgeons is on their bucket list.

All in all, I'm slightly overwhelmed but excited. The world of plastic surgery has proven to be more interesting than I expected.

Astor seems to prefer to block out the majority of his day, only taking a few patients. I didn't ask why, and he didn't seem willing to share. But the point is, I managed to forget my run-in with Dr. Potter, keeping pace while Astor told me everything he wanted me to know about Potter's Plastics.

Until now.

"Halle, could you grab a notepad and come in here please?"

Looking up from a chart I'm putting together, I swallow. "But sir. It's your…"

Those dark brown eyes gleam with mischief. "I struggle with retaining information," he lies, pushing the door wider, revealing Dr. Potter in one of the wingback chairs, his foot resting casually over his knee.

But I know Dr. Potter is anything but relaxed. I can tell by the tension in his arms and the muscle ticking over his jaw.

"This won't take long," Astor lies with an adorable wink. "I promise."

Dr. Potter has steered clear of me all morning, after what we'll call bathroom-gate. I called Serena after learning how to work Astor's calendar and gave her the available times that he could meet with Dr. Astor. She huffed, but chose noon and hung up on me. Fortunately, Astor left his outside door open, so I didn't have to see Dr. Potter go in, but now, he wants me to join them for a meeting that likely pertains to me.

Grabbing my notebook, I stand, inhaling a calming breath.

I should have never mouthed off to Dr. Potter earlier this morning, but he flips something inside me like no other man has ever done before. And trust me when I say men have caused a multitude of bullshit to flip my bitch switch, but not like Dr. Potter. Dr. Potter makes me lose all sense of composure.

But I can handle this meeting and this job. Because no matter what Dr. Potter does, I can become his friend. I have to. I need this procedure. "Sure thing, Dr. Astor."

Astor holds the door as I brush past him, keeping my eyes on the angry ass in the chair. Even though I'm choosing to play nice, it does not mean I'm a coward. Dr. Potter will not intimidate me.

Well, he does intimidate me, but he'll never know he does.

"Okay, Vance. The floor is yours." Astor closes the door as I sit in the chair next to Vance, keeping my eyes on Astor as he leans against his desk.

The room is silent, and I swear I can just make out the sounds of someone counting.

"Van—"

"I don't want her working here," Vance blurts out, cutting off Astor.

I hold on to the pen, not bothering to write it down. Vance not wanting me here isn't news to me or Astor.

"I'm sorry you feel that way, Vance," starts Astor, a big, stupid grin on his face. "But, unfortunately, I need a secretary, and your brother ran my last one off. I suggest you take up this issue with him."

Vance doesn't even flinch. "Pick someone else."

"No."

Suddenly, the room feels smaller as the two men stare at each other, a silent war raging between them.

"It's unprofessional," is all Vance manages to grit out between clenched teeth.

"What's unprofessional, brother, is you giving consults but not scheduling any surgeries."

I suck in a breath, and Vance's gaze flicks to me before focusing back on his brother. "Since when have you been monitoring my surgery schedule?"

Astor doesn't miss a beat. "Since you haven't gone back into the operating room in a year. Insurance reimbursement is down. We're not bringing in the revenue to sustain the practice. I want to know why you aren't doing surgeries."

Dr. Potter hasn't been doing surgeries? In a year?

Vance stands, shoving the chair back harshly, causing it to topple over. "This is fucking ridiculous. Keep your secretary, just stay away from my patients." The way he says patients, all warm and protective, like they mean everything to him guts me as Vance storms out, slamming the door behind him.

For a moment, it seems as if the entire office is silent, absorbing this revelation. Dr. Potter hasn't performed any of his surgeries in months.

"What's wrong with him?" I whisper, hoping I'm not crossing the line of professionalism by asking.

Astor sighs, coming over and righting the chair. "I don't know. He won't talk to us about it."

"You wanting me to come work for you wasn't so I could convince him to perform my surgery, was it?"

The lines in Astor's forehead crinkle. "Partly."

"And the other part?"

A smile tugs at his lips before he frowns. "You've been the only one besides us who's been able to elicit any emotion out of him. I was hoping whatever was silencing him, you'd be able to break."

"And if I can't break whatever it is?"

Astor shrugs, the concerned pinch of his brows worrying me. "Then we both can say we tried, right?"

His words echo in my head. At least we tried.

And ultimately, that's what I wanted.

A chance.

And with this new information, I might just get one. Dr. Potter's decision not to do my surgery might not have anything to do with me after all.

Hope blooms in my chest as I flash a renewed smile at the eldest Potter. "We'll go down trying."

CHAPTER SEVEN

Halle

When five o'clock finally rolls around, I've filed a bazillion charts and spent two hours on the phone with potential patients, just like myself, who are desperate to get on Astor's calendar. I learned that Dr. Duke's specialty is cosmetic surgery, aka, his favorite, boobs.

Dr. Astor is a craniomaxillofacial surgeon, who is most sought after by moms and their infants with cleft palates. Dr. Potter, I already know, is a burn surgeon, who is known to reconstruct and repair traumatic scars. All three brothers' calendars stay booked, which keeps the office revolving with constant patients throughout the day. Some crying tears of joy and others tears of sadness.

I don't know what disqualifies patients from surgery, but I would guess people like myself who had a bad experience with anesthesia or the fact some injuries just cannot be fixed. I don't know which of those Dr. Potter claims is his problem with doing my surgery, but I truly hope he reconsiders. Soon.

"You need anything else?" I pop my head into Astor's office.

He covers the mouthpiece of the phone in his other hand. "Nope. I'm good. I'll see you tomorrow, yeah?"

He's been worried that Vance hurt my feelings at the meeting. I didn't tell him Vance hurt my feelings more in the bathroom than in the meeting. I simply reassured him that I was tougher than I looked. No matter what Dr. Potter throws at me, I can handle it because I'd do anything for a new beginning at this thing called life.

"Yep, I'll be here bright and early," I assure Astor.

He flashes me a wink. "Attagirl."

I wave the crazy man off and disappear down the hall. After the horrible lunch meeting and bathroom-gate, I haven't spotted Dr. Potter again. Which, if I'm being honest, is a relief. It wouldn't feel right to be snarky to him now that I know something is really going on with him.

What could possibly be happening that would cause him not to perform surgeries? The article I read years ago made it out like Dr. Potter lived and breathed for the OR. Whatever it is, it seems to worry both of his brothers enough that they're willing to do anything to snap him out of it.

I spot Serena at the nurses' office and attempt to play nice since she hasn't. "Have a good evening, Serena. See you tomorrow."

Her eyes roll, and she turns around as if wishing me a good evening would cause her to explode. It very well might. Her pantsuit is tight enough that keeping in all that bitchiness is probably a massive strain on the buttons. It's whatever, though. I learned a long time ago that if you put all your faith in people, you'll only end up disappointed.

Yet, I did it with Dr. Potter.

But I don't have to allow Serena to have that power over me. I don't care what she thinks, nor do I need her to wish me a good evening. I will have a good evening on my own with my new job and new paycheck.

The remaining five grand I need for my surgery is finally within reach.

When I'm out of the building, I locate the bus stop just to the right of the parking garage for Potter's Plastics. I would have loved to live close enough so I could save bus fare, but Clyde's is at least six miles from Dr. Potter's office. My hips would last less than a quarter of a mile before they gave out and caused me to cave to the pain.

"Hey," I greet the man already waiting on the bus bench. "You mind if I sit next to you?"

He replies with a sweet smile. "Not at all, little lady."

I figured, but just in case, I felt like it couldn't hurt to break the ice, and my mama taught me to always be friendly. You never know if someone is a murderer. Being nice just might save you from being their next victim.

And it's the right thing to do. There are too many assholes in this world already. It doesn't need another one.

Sitting down, I situate my purse on my lap and lean back, letting my eyes drift shut just a little. With a long day and minimal sleep, I can already feel the exhaustion setting in. Who knew working at an office doing administrative stuff all day would wear someone out?

Well, that and I had a drink at lunch with my neighbor, too. I'm sure the small amount of alcohol is contributing to the tiredness. But Neighbor-Who-Doesn't-Have-A-Name insisted we celebrate my new job by taking me to this little bistro down the road from the office. The inside was decorated in southern décor, these cute little Mason jars hanging from the ceiling with white tea candles inside, casting this warm glow over the quaint tables with big sitting chairs.

He made me try this burger with the egg on the patty, claiming it was the best burger Texas had to offer. Honestly, I gagged a little when I saw it, but my young neighbor assured me it tasted better than it looked. And he was right.

We ended up spending two hours at lunch at which point I panicked and ran with my shoes in my hand and begged for Astor's forgiveness. Which wasn't hard to get, considering all Astor did was laugh and wave away my concern. He didn't even realize I had left.

Honestly, I think Astor could live without a secretary. For the most part, he seems organized and maintains personal relationships with most of his patients. They call his cell, and after speaking with them, he tells me what appointment time to put them down for.

It was clear he didn't require my assistance, which makes me think that his easy demeanor regarding Vance is covering the true concern he really

feels. Whatever plagues Vance plagues his brothers, too.

But what if Vance never recovers? What if he never goes back to the operating room? What if he never agrees to my revision surgery?

My stomach rolls at the thought of all this being for nothing. It was my only thought, my only goal for years, and it could all come to a crashing halt.

I think of Vance on the bathroom floor earlier, beautifully broken. His threat echoing in my mind.

He wasn't my savior. Not anymore.

Inhaling, I look to the sky. I don't need a savior. I've already saved myself. All I need is a blank slate, and if Dr. Potter can't provide one, I'll find someone else. Nothing and no one will come between me and my future again.

"Halle!" Tires squeal and I jerk my head up and look to my right, finding a black sports car with the window down.

Is that? No way. It can't be.

"Dr. Potter?" I finally call out, confused.

I can't be sure, but I think his eyes roll. "What the *fuck* are you doing?"

What am I doing?

I look at the man on the bench with me. "This is the bus stop, right?" He nods his confirmation, and I turn back to Dr. Potter.

"It's after five, and Astor said I could leave," I tell him, just in case he's confused about who I work for again.

Dr. Potter rakes a frustrated hand through his hair as another car pulls up behind him and blows the horn, which he aptly ignores. "Do you not drive?" The way he asks the question seems like it pained him to get the words out.

"I drive," I tell him matter-of-factly.

He scoffs out this rude and totally uncalled-for noise. "So, you just decided to take the bus today?" Another horn blows, but Vance still doesn't look back. He seems intently focused on my reason for sitting on the bus stop bench.

"Correct," I grit out. Gone is the nice girl from a few minutes ago. I don't owe Vance a freaking explanation. Especially since he doesn't bother explaining anything to me, either. He can take his demands and shove them where the sun doesn't shine. "You have a good evening," I add, giving Vance a little wave goodbye.

Hopefully, he takes it as a hint and leaves. I think I've had about all I can take of his attitude today.

The horn-blower in the car behind him finally has had enough and yells for Vance to move his car, which Vance does not do. Instead, he mumbles something I don't catch, tugging at his hair until he exhales, offering me a tight smile. "You have ten seconds to get in the car."

"Are you serious?"

Maybe he hit his head in the bathroom?

But then, he starts counting. "Ten...Nine..."

CHAPTER EIGHT

Vance

She stares at me like I've just asked her to come back to my room for a quickie. "Did you hear me?"

The last thing I needed today was to find this sweet, southern belle on the bus bench, two seconds from getting mugged by the resident pickpocket.

"I heard you," she finally snaps, showing that she was, in fact, just choosing not to do what I asked.

"Do I need to help you from the bench, or would you like to walk?" I don't have time for her theatrics right now. Nor do I feel like taking her home when all I want to do is get as far away from her as I can. But she helped me earlier. Who knows how long I would have been out without her waking me.

It would have been much worse had Astor or Duke found me. They would have gone all doctor on me, and I would have ended up with another therapist and an emergency room visit.

I owe Ms. Belle for waking me, even if I would have preferred anyone other than her.

"Are you threatening me, Dr. Potter?" She looks shocked, and I'm not sure why. Have I given this woman any impression that I'm a nice guy?

"Absolutely not. But I can assist you off the bench if you need help."

I'm not opposed to dealing with this situation quickly. I don't have the headspace for being patient.

As if she knew I would enjoy "helping" her, Halle gathers her purse, speaks to the criminal, and walks slowly to the other side of my car, taking her sweet ass time opening the door before sitting in the passenger seat.

I barely give her time to buckle up before I peel onto the street, fury weighing down the pedal before I realize I'm heading to my house, having no idea where Halle lives. "What street?"

The air inside the car thickens with tension.

"I asked you a question, Ms. Belle."

"And I'm refusing to answer. Sometimes, Dr. Potter, we don't get what we want. You barked at me to get into the car. You should have known you didn't know where I lived before you offered the ride."

I have half the mind to slam on the brakes and put her out on the sidewalk. "Ms. Belle, my patience is dwindling."

I chance a look in her direction and notice she's staring out the passenger window, a slow, deviant smile tugging against her lips. "Seems like lots of things are dwindling." She turns to me, nothing but southern sass in her tone. "Like sleep, maybe?"

"We're not discussing earlier," I clip.

"So, we're just supposed to act like nothing ever happened in the bathroom?"

"Yes." My fingers flex along the wheel as I keep driving straight ahead. "I won't ask you again. What street?"

She seems to ponder her situation for a minute while staring out the window, taking in the sights.

"Halle."

She turns slowly. "Halle?"

For fuck's sake. "That's your name, isn't it?"

She shrugs, her small shoulders delicate under the thin material. "You called me Peach earlier." She arches a brow and I look away.

"You misunderstood. I didn't call you Peach."

A light rumbling comes from her throat. "You're such a liar. You called me Peach. In the bathroom, when you were all growly and threatening me."

She makes it sound like I was a stray dog growling over a burrito wrapper. "Now, you're just making things up."

I did call her Peach. I don't know why the name came to me. Perhaps I was still dazed from the blackout, or maybe I simply forgot her name. It wouldn't be the first time I'd forgotten someone's name.

"Why, Dr. Potter, are you blushing?"

I can feel the heat on my face. Why does she incite this reaction from me? I'm known to be patient and focused. Dealing with people is my specialty. This woman, however, seems to see through my shield and is brave enough to call me out on it.

Grinding down on my teeth, I grit out the demand again. "Your address."

Like my impatience is just what she needed after a long day at the office, she chuckles. "Fine. I'll tell you my address, Dr. Grouch."

"Great." The sooner she's gone, the faster I can get home and drown this day away in bourbon.

"I live at 444 I can't help you."

It's not so much the words that cause me to slam on the brakes but the snort she lets out after saying those words.

"You think this is funny?" I whip into a parking spot on the side of the street.

"Yes, actually." She laughs again, searching for something on the door. "No one told you to force me into your car."

My jaw throbs as I try calming my breathing. The last thing I need is to pass out again. "You don't know this city," I try explaining calmly. "Or the man who sat next to you on the bench."

Her brows furrow. "He seemed nice enough."

A laugh that lacks sincerity bursts out of me. "Oh, he is. Until he's lifted your wallet."

She thinks about my words for a moment and then shrugs her delicate shoulders. "Oh, well, he probably needs the money more than I do. Besides, he wouldn't get but a few bucks anyway."

And this is why she needed a ride home. "I realize you're from a tiny town in Georgia, where the worst thing that happens to people is a flat tire, but here, you need to be more aware of your surroundings. You're too trusting."

Those wisps of blonde locks framing her face distract me when she turns, a few strands of hair getting stuck at the corner of her plump lips.

"Thanks for the helpful tip, Dr. Potter, but you know jack shit about me or my hometown."

She finally finds what she's looking for, the lock, and pulls it up, snatching her purse and getting out of the car. "I can take care of myself." She slams the car door, but then, that sweet southerner kicks in, and she looks to the sky before adding, "Have a great evening, Dr. Potter. I'll see you tomorrow."

I could call a board meeting and have her dismissed as an employee. Astor knows it's unprofessional to have Halle working there, but the determination in her eyes as she offers me a small wave sparks a level of curiosity I didn't know I had. Even if she's scared or disappointed, she powers through, determined to reach whatever goal she has in that sweet little head of hers.

Letting the window down, I try asking politely through clenched teeth, "Get back in the car."

She gives me her back. "It's okay, I can walk from here. My place isn't that far."

Dammit if she doesn't piss me off in seconds. "I wasn't asking."

"Sure, you were, Dr. Potter. Bye!"

Fuck it.

I get out of the car and manage to catch up with her in a few strides, slipping my arms around her legs and tossing her over my shoulder in one motion.

"What are you doing?" she screams, her skirt blowing partly in my face. "Put me down!"

I realize I've now crossed over into unprofessionalism with this event, not to mention every single time I'm in front of Ms. Belle, but I can't seem to manage to find the professional Dr. Potter when I'm around her. "I'll put you down when you can do as you're told and get in the car."

"You don't tell me what to do!" She kicks her legs, and I tighten my hold against the back of her thighs.

"It's my responsibility to look out for my employees," I lie.

The scoff she lets out only tightens my grip. "I work for your brother, not you."

"Everyone works for me," I growl. "Everyone." She need not know the inner workings of our practice but suffice it to say, it is mine. Every inch.

We approach the car, and I manage to open the car door one-handed. "Are you going to get in the car, or do I need to help you with that, too?"

She considers her options for a moment and finally lets out a sigh and relaxes against me. "I'll get in."

Thank fuck.

Easing her down the front of my body, her softness against my hardness sends chills against my skin. "Thank you," I manage when she bends, sitting in the seat with a rogue smile.

"Did that physically hurt you to say?"

No sense in lying to her. "Yes." And then I slam the door, locking her in until I can get to the driver's side and get situated, taking several deep breaths to calm my racing heart. "Let's try this again," I start. "Ms. Belle, I would like to give you a ride home, so you don't get pickpocketed on the bus."

"How very nice of you, Dr. Potter. Do you do this for all of your employees?"

It's like she loves pissing me off. "No, actually. I tend to hire employees with more self-preservation."

Immediately, I feel shitty after saying the words. Truth is, I don't give a shit how my employees get home, but I know from Ms. Belle's chart, she's lived on a farm in a small town in Georgia. This is likely her first time in a big city. A city in which she came to alone, in search of me. I feel responsible that she gets home safely. I would have preferred she'd taken a plane home a week ago after our appointment, but since she seems determined to stay here, I feel like the least I can do is make sure she makes it back home in one piece, especially after today.

"Well, my apologies for failing to meet your expectations, but I really can take care of myself."

Her tone has changed, and I know I've hurt her feelings.

I sigh. "Look—"

"Don't. I don't want your pity."

She leaves it unsaid that she wants on my schedule, and I told her no. But even if I manage to go back into the operating room, I won't be able to perform the surgery.

I pull out into traffic, headed in any direction at this point. "It's not pity I'm offering. I meant what I said at the appointment. I have colleagues that would be happy to review your case. Just because I can't perform your surgery, doesn't mean someone else won't."

She sits quietly for a moment before she speaks. "I don't want anyone else."

The constant ache in my chest grips me in a powerful hold. "I'm sorry. I wish I could help you."

She turns her face away, and I catch a glimpse of her rubbing at her face. "33 Sunville Drive."

"Pardon?"

She turns back, and I see the redness in her eyes. "That's where I'm staying until you agree to be my surgeon."

CHAPTER NINE

Halle

If I thought Dr. Potter would respond to my comment about staying until he agreed to be my doctor, I would have been wrong. He simply swallowed, that muscle twitching in his jaw the whole way until the motel came into view.

That's when I finally got a different reaction.

"Do you have the correct address?" he asks me, slowing as we get closer to the motel.

"Yep, this is me." I point to the room facing the road, my no-name neighbor already outside in his plastic chair, taking a long drag on his cigarette. "You can let me out here."

He makes a noise in his throat that sounds a lot like *the hell*.

"Really, I'm staying here." I point just as he passes the entrance. "You missed the turn." I try not to sound annoyed since technically he's giving me a ride—a ride I did not need or want.

"I have an errand," he grumbles while his knuckles turn white along the steering wheel.

"Well," I scoff. "Don't let my kidnapping interfere with the rest of your evening. I can wait. It's not like I haven't had a long day dealing with assholes." I give him a pointed look, so he knows that one of the "assholes" I referenced includes him—and his secretary, but I'm blaming him for her behavior, too. One is not born an asshole, it develops, and I imagine working for Dr. Dick here isn't without consequences.

Vance keeps his eyes on the road. I swear he doesn't even blink. The only way I know he's still alive is the fact that hot, annoying muscle in his jaw ticks in a perfect rhythm. It's quite amazing he can stay still otherwise.

Finally, after several minutes of me staring, he finally sighs and tosses a bored glance my way. "I didn't kidnap you."

Yeah, I laugh. "What do you call this then?"

He faces forward, refusing to answer, which is fine because I'm right. Though, I don't understand why he bothered. Dr. Potter was quick to push me out of his office with crushed dreams, so why does it matter if I take the bus home? He made it clear he couldn't help me. I assume that means with transportation as well.

We drive, and I take a minute to enjoy the beautiful scenery that I've yet to see since I've been in Bloomfield, Texas. I've been so focused on getting back on Dr. Potter's schedule and securing a job, I haven't bothered wasting money on extra bus fare to see any sights.

"Is this your first time in another state?"

His voice pulls me from the big oak canopies. "No."

The slight tilt to his mouth pisses me off. "No?"

The arch of his brows dares me to lie again, but instead of validating his theory, I give him the partial truth. "This is my first time in Texas."

"Shocker."

It'd be terribly tacky if I punched him, right? In his own asshole way, he's being a nice guy and not letting me ride home with a thief. But he's got a lot of work to do when it comes to dealing with humans. His clipped, broody yet jerk vibe isn't ideal for the average person. Seriously.

"Well, unlike you, I'm not falling asleep with a full bank account and belly."

The words were out before I could stop them, but I didn't want him thinking I'm some dumb country girl who hasn't experienced life and other states. Well, I haven't experienced life, that part is true, but I'm not dumb. I couldn't help that my college years were spent in physical therapy rather than a frat house. I didn't ask for my adversity, but I was stuck with it, nonetheless. I'm making the best of the situation, and I don't need some hoity physician looking down on me in his fancy sports car.

"Just stop here." I sigh, noting the car slowing down. "I can walk the rest of the way." I ignore his wide eyes and clenching jaw. "Seriously, Dr. Potter. Neither of us has the energy to deal with each other right now. Stop the car."

I just need my bed and a long conversation with Oscar. He'll understand the day I've had. He's the one who's endured every job I started and quit. It's been a long, few years of saving money for this surgery. A long, few years of learning to walk again, spilling drinks on customers because I was still rebuilding my arm strength. The whispers were the worst. No matter how far away I thought I'd gone, the rumors always followed me. *Did you hear what happened to her? I heard she tried to stab him. No, I heard she was breaking into his house.*

Over and over, I relived my past trauma. I powered through, and for what reason? So Dr. Potter could make me feel like that same small girl who was talked about? The same girl that couldn't leave her room because she was ugly and weak. Because she allowed a man to break her.

I'll never be that girl again.

He won't break me.

No matter what mistakes I've made, I've paid for them.

This Halle is changed. She's stronger than ever before. She doesn't need a man. She only needs a chance to go after the life she wanted. A life to be anyone she wants to be. A mermaid. A rich mistress. I can be anyone in front of a camera. I never have to be Halle from Georgia with the limp and scars.

No one knows this Halle.

This Halle is endless.

"Are you hungry?" comes a quiet voice.

I shake my head, there's no need to face him. "No, I just want to go home. Please take me home, Vance."

I hate the strain in my voice, the way it broke at the end, showing my weakness. The last thing I need is Dr. Potter seeing a limitation. I don't need him saying I'm not mentally ready for surgery or that I'm not strong enough to handle going under the knife again. I've seen therapists. Dozens. Trust me, I can handle it.

The car slows and Vance turns around at the next gas station.

"Thank you," I tell him quietly, the exhaustion of dealing with this day settling in as the motel comes into view. I don't think I've ever been so happy to see the rundown sign with letters y and s missing.

It might look like a shithole to Vance, but to me, it feels safe and like home. Not like the home I ran from in Georgia. I don't need fresh paint and fake neighbors. I just need four walls and Oscar.

And maybe my grouchy teenage neighbor. He's not afraid to be himself around me.

We pull into Clyde's, and my hand is on the handle, ready to jump out as soon as Vance stops the car. But when he puts the car in park, and the doors unlock, he relocks them. "Can I come in and use the bathroom?"

He asks the question so nonchalantly, I would have believed he needed to actually use the bathroom if his forehead didn't wrinkle while he scoured the parking lot as if someone was about to leap out and pull a gun on us.

"You don't need to use the restroom," I accuse. "You just want to see how shitty my place is."

His gaze turns hard as his eyes narrow in my direction. "How do you know I don't need to pee?"

"Because you don't." I lean back in the leather seat and fold my arms across my chest, challenging him.

"Should I prove it by peeing on your door then?" he suggests, seriously.

Dammit, I laugh. I don't mean to. The last thing Dr. Potter needs is encouragement. "I'm tempted to call bullshit."

Vance's gaze doesn't waver. "But you won't because that's not what sweet, southern women do, is it?"

Ugh! I want to shake him. Just full-on shake the meanness out of him. Instead, I answer him like he does me. "Who says I'm a sweet girl?"

He flashes me a wink and grins, unlocking the door, presumably taking my comment as a win. "You did, Peach. When you helped me in the bathroom earlier."

He gets out of the car, and I scramble out behind him. "I thought we weren't bringing up bathroom-gate."

He rears back, a line forming across his forehead. "What the hell is bathroom-gate?"

Oh, geez.

I wave my hand between us, pushing him over so I can unlock the door. "Just hurry and use the bathroom."

Opening the door, the stench of stale cigarettes and old carpet hits us in the face.

"Charming," Vance mutters, pushing in with a scowl, stopping just inside the door, taking in my made-up bed and overnight bag that has spilled out on top of the quilt. The handles on the dresser drawers are broken, otherwise, my clothes would be folded in there so Vance didn't get an eyeful of my underwear and support braces.

I scramble across the room and start shoving stuff back into the bag, pointing to the far end of the room. "The bathroom is there. You'll need to shove hard to get the door to close."

Pausing, Vance gives me one more cursory look before making his way to the bathroom. And like I suggested, he puts his shoulder into the door, closing it with a bang.

When he's no longer smothering me with his presence, I slump back onto the bed and exhale. What a crazy day. What a crazy week. Never would I have imagined that this mission to get on Dr. Potter's schedule would have gone so sideways. And this ride home? What was that all about? It almost feels like Dr. Potter is Dr. Jekyll and Mr. Hyde. His hot and cold behavior is exhausting. I can't decide if he's a dick or a good man like the article suggested. He's hard to read, and that's unfortunate. I already have terrible men-reading skills—I failed at the last one. I don't need another test I can't pass.

I don't know if I can handle it emotionally.

The bathroom door opens, and Vance comes out with wide eyes, his thumb pointing over his shoulder. "You don't have hot water." He blinks slowly. "And there's a fish in your sink."

I don't bother sitting up. My body is exhausted to the core. I just need to lie here for a day or so. "I have hot water," I correct. "You just have to give it ten minutes." I wave it off like it's the least of my worries.

"Ten minutes?" He sounds offended but, fortunately, doesn't address the fish issue.

Staring up at the ceiling, I grin. "I know it's probably hard for you to understand, but sometimes, us regular people have to wait on things." I pause, hearing his steps come closer. "I hear it builds character."

The bed dips, and I turn, finding Vance eyeing me. "Are you really planning to stay here until I perform your surgery?"

His voice is dangerously low, his eyes weighted with something like anger.

"Yes, I'm not taking no for an answer."

Vance's throat bobs, his jaw tight with tension. "Let me call a colleague. I promise—"

I don't give him time to finish. "It has to be you. No one but you."

He releases a breath, raking his hands through his hair. "Halle..." He says my name like it's painful. "I want to help you, I do. And I know you don't believe me, but I can't do your surgery. It's too risky."

"It's not," I argue. "The last surgeon I spoke to said with proper monitoring and an experienced surgeon, I would have a good possibility of success."

"A possibility," he reiterates. "Not a promise. You could die on the table. Why risk it?"

I sit up and face the man who is the only roadblock between me and my future career in show business. "Because these scars no longer define me. I want new opportunities, not a reminder of the past."

CHAPTER
TEN

Halle

Two weeks later, I'm finding a routine at Potter's Plastics.

Vance shows up at the motel first thing, every morning, demanding I accept his pity ride to the office.

We argue and end up late for work.

At five, he stands in the doorway of my office, his briefcase in hand, insisting it's time to leave.

We argue more.

I don't get home until six, at which point, I ask him if he's ready to take on my case. He says no, and I go inside.

Rinse and repeat. Every. Single. Day.

We're at a stalemate.

I am no closer to getting on Vance's schedule than I was three weeks ago. At this point, even I doubt my abilities of persistence. Maybe it's time I consider another surgeon. After all, the goal is a blank slate, a fresh start. Vance may have been the one to inspire that decision, but he isn't the only surgeon around.

I need to find someone just as credentialed and willing. Which is how I find myself confiding in Duke in one of the exam rooms. Astor was at a meeting, and since I was all caught up, I insisted on helping.

"Vance likes you," he muses. "He's never given an employee a ride to work before."

I knew it was never about that employee satisfaction crap.

I scoff. "He thinks I'm naive and can't manage to take the bus without getting murdered."

Duke flashes me an adorable grin. "I doubt that."

I suck in a breath, the pain a little worse today since it's raining. "He feels bad that I won't leave until he does the surgery."

Duke's head cocks to the side. "He's still saying no?"

"He insists another colleague will take my case, but not him." I toy with my shirt. "I think I'm going to take his offer and consult with another surgeon. I don't know if I can wait any longer, and I'm ready to move on."

Dark eyebrows that should not be blessed to a man, furrow. "Did he mention the surgeon's name?"

I shake my head. "Nope, but I almost have the money now, so whatever surgeon he gives me, I'll be able to afford the procedure soon."

Duke drags a finger across his bottom lip, worrying it. "You asked Vance again last night?"

I like how he doesn't call his brother Dr. Potter, rather referring to him by his first name. It humanizes the scary Dr. Potter—enough that when Duke speaks of him, it sounds like we're discussing a mutual friend and not the man who gave me a flat, "No," a few weeks ago and threw me out of his office, crushing my dreams underneath his expensive loafers.

I shrug and turn to stock the cabinet. The pain from Vance's decision is still very raw. "Yep."

"And he said no?"

I'm not sure why Duke seems so surprised. Vance has been clear from the beginning about not taking me on.

"He did," I answer quietly, blowing out a breath. "I shouldn't have insulted him during the appointment with the layaway comment." I finally look up and meet Duke's confused gaze. "It was inappropriate."

"It was hilarious." He tips his chin at my body, still grinning. "Where are the scars you want revised?"

"Uh… on my legs… my hips, too."

Duke studies me a moment as if he could see through my clothes. "Can I see them?"

A knot forms in my throat, but I swallow past it. "Sure." He's a doctor after all. Surely, he won't be like his brother. Maybe I made an appointment with the wrong Dr. Potter.

Nodding, Dr. Duke takes a gown from the stack on the counter and hands it over. "When you've finished changing, knock on the door, and I'll come back in."

My voice is barely a whisper. "Okay."

In a matter of seconds, Dr. Duke is gone, and I'm left standing in the empty exam room. My stomach clenches, and it suddenly feels hard to breathe. With Dr. Duke looking at the scars… does that mean he would agree to do the revision? I mean, he and his brother are equally credentialed plastic surgeons. Granted, they each have different specialties, but Dr. Duke is still a plastic surgeon. No matter how many cases he's done, he could make the scars less noticeable.

Anything would be better than the scars left by the trauma surgeons.

And I would be achieving my goal.

That's what I came here for. It's what I've worked toward for so many years. Maybe I was wrong letting Vance delay my dreams. Just because life doesn't go as I think it should, it doesn't mean it's the wrong move.

A flutter of excitement quickly replaces the nerves as I strip down and change into a gown and knock on the door. And like a good doctor, Duke waits a minute so I can get to the exam table and situate myself before he opens the door and flashes me an easy-going smile.

"I'm no Vance, but if it makes you feel more comfortable, I can scowl and not speak to you while I do the exam," he teases, pushing the door closed.

"That's okay," I chuckle. "I'm not nervous."

Duke approaches with a file in his hands. "I don't suppose you are. A crush injury and six months in the hospital will do that to a person."

Nodding, I offer him a half smile. Being used to strangers seeing me naked might be something I've grown accustomed to but being confident in that body is another issue entirely.

"You want to start by showing me the worst scar?"

I like that he's giving me the control here. It feels less like an exam and more like swapping scar stories with a friend. "Sure. It's this one on my—"

The door wrenches open, and I quickly pull the gown back in place.

"What the fuck are you doing?"

I know the owner of those angry words before I can even lift my head, and by the grin on Duke's face, so does he.

Oh no. "I was just—"

Vance's gaze sears me where I sit, pointing harshly with one finger. "I'm not talking to you."

Duke flashes me a wink and squares his shoulders, turning slowly to face his brother. "Dr. Potter, I'm with a patient. If you'll wait in my office, I will be with you in a moment."

My heart sinks when Vance pushes the door closed, the soft click of the latch being the only noise in the room. "Ms. Belle is my patient." His voice is nothing but gravel as he steps up to his brother.

His fury doesn't seem to do anything but amuse Dr. Duke as he cocks his head to the side. "I recall you declined to take her case."

For a brief moment, Dr. Potter flicks his gaze to mine before he levels Duke with a glare that would have most grown men cowering in a corner.

"Did I mistake your note in the chart, Dr. Potter?"

Come on, Duke, don't taunt him.

Vance's jaw clenches, but he stays silent.

A silence that Duke clearly doesn't heed. "There are two other surgeons in this office. Ms. Belle is entitled to have a second opinion." The unspoken words *since you declined* hang tensely in the air between the brothers. "Now, if you'll wait in my office, I'll be with you in a—"

"You're not doing the revision." Dr. Potter's voice is thick, his throat pulsing as he struggles to keep himself in check.

Duke chuckles, seemingly enjoying this exchange with his brother, and takes a step forward, pushing into Vance's chest. "You seem to have forgotten a few of those policies you hold on to closely." He straightens Vance's tie, mockingly. "Let me remind you that clause 3.1b says that if one surgeon declines a case, the patient is free to consult another in the same practice. Now," he taps his chest, "brief me on my new patient."

The two men stand nose to nose, neither saying a word until Duke adds, "Unless you've reconsidered Ms. Belle's case."

Without looking at me, Vance holds his brother's gaze with a glare more severe than third-degree burns. "Patient is a twenty-three-year-old female with a crush injury post hit and run."

Vance steps to the side and approaches the table. "Please lie back, Ms. Belle."

Part of me would rather sprint from this room and drive back to Georgia, but then there's this other part that is actually curious to see Dr. Potter in action. This is the furthest he's ever gotten to an actual examination.

Lying back, the paper on the table crinkles beneath me as I focus on the ceiling, feeling Dr. Duke approach the other side of the table. I'm lying trapped between two warring brothers, who just so happen to be the best plastic surgeons in Texas. It's a position Serena most certainly dreams of.

"I'm sorry, my hands are cold," Vance mutters.

Pulling my gaze from the ceiling to where the pressure of his palms lie against my thigh, I grin. "Who knew the devil would have cold hands."

Dr. Potter's mouth twitches, but he never allows himself to smile. Instead, he holds my gaze as his fingers curl around the gown, dragging it up my leg to my hip, where the worst of the scars reside.

I gasp, the cool air hitting the space between my legs like an arctic wind. Lying here like a sacrifice, my body a mere exhibit for this man, I try not to focus on what he sees. Jagged, pink and white puffy skin that was stretched and stitched together like Frankenstein himself had his way with me.

Chancing a look at Vance, I'm met with horror as his throat works, his eyes pinched shut as if he can't stand to look at me. His reaction shouldn't bother me as much as it does, but I guess I expected more of a flat reaction from the infamous Dr. Potter. Surely, he's seen worse, but his heavy breaths indicate otherwise.

"Your report, Dr. Potter," Duke demands, his voice in full control.

Vance's fingers tighten on the gown, and he takes a deep breath before his green eyes flash open. Like a switch was flipped, he begins rattling off a bunch of clinical jargon I don't bother paying attention to. I've heard enough over the years. I don't need to hear the man who's disgusted by the mere sight of my body tell his brother what all is wrong with me.

Closing my eyes, I tune him out while Duke interrupts him with questions here and there. It isn't until Duke laughs that I open my eyes and pay attention.

"What do you mean I don't need a better look?"

Vance's hands tremble against me. "I showed you the worst of them. Believe me when I say, her case is out of your scope of expertise."

Duke chuckles and rounds the opposite side of the table, where Vance lingers like a dark gargoyle standing guard. "I beg to differ. I'll decide what's in my scope after a thorough examination. Now, step aside, Dr. Potter."

Vance doesn't move. Instead, he tugs the gown over the exposed part of my body. "A good surgeon would have been able to determine the severity of her scars from a mile away. You're not qualified."

Duke flashes me a smile. "Halle, would you mind coming back tomorrow? About three-thirty? I think Dr. Potter has a meeting and won't be able to be a deterrent then."

I swear Vance growls.

"Does that work for you? Obviously, I'll get Astor to approve the time off."

Watching Vance as he stares at something across the room, I nod. "Yeah, that—"

"I'll take your case."

I suck in a breath at Dr. Potter's abrupt words.

"I..." Shock steals my thought process. But then the word "no" reminds me of all the times he turned me down. "I want Dr. Duke," I say firmly and am rewarded when his hateful gaze snaps down to glare at me.

"Too bad. You get me or no one. Dr. Duke isn't qualified to take on a case like yours."

I shrug. "I'll risk it."

Duke makes a noise that I ignore. I don't have the energy to figure out his reaction since I'm elbow-deep in arguing with his exasperating brother.

"You won't risk it. You'll allow me to perform the surgery, or you'll go back home to Georgia and find a surgeon there."

The annoying tic in Vance's jaw sets my nerves on fire. How dare he! "Oh, so *now* you'll take on my case?" I sit up and yank the gown from his grip and stand. "Excuse me while I don't give a shit. I don't want a surgeon who can't stand to look at me."

Tears threaten to fall, and suddenly, I'm exhausted. Tired of fighting the pain of insecurity. Tired of feeling like I don't look like everyone else. I just want normality, and anything that Dr. Potter touches is nothing less than perfect. It's blatantly obvious why he doesn't want my case. He can't make me perfect.

Backing away, I grab the doorknob and yank the door open wide. "I'd like to get dressed now."

Duke is the first to leave, placing his hand on my shoulder. "I'm sorry."

I don't look at him when I say, "It's not your fault."

It's Vance's.

"Dr. Potter?" I prompt when he just stands there, eyes hard, jaw clenched. "I need to get back to work."

If anything should make him move, it will be knowing I'm on the clock and not working as he so loves to remind me. But he still doesn't move.

"Dr. Potter. I'd like to get dressed," I repeat.

The annoyance in my tone must clue him in to how much I appreciate him crashing the only consult I've had since he rudely turned me down because his feet move him to the door. But I should have known he wouldn't go quietly. "Tell Serena to fit you into tomorrow's schedule for a proper consult."

This man. "I already told you. I want Dr.—"

"I'll see you tomorrow." He closes the door behind him, and I'm left with a terrible urge to chase after him and scream. But I don't. Because Dr. Potter might run this office, but he doesn't run me.

CHAPTER ELEVEN

Vance

"Are you fucking kidding me, Duke? Entering a patient's room without a witness! We could be sued. Again."

I slam the door to my office and narrow my gaze at the pain in my ass perched on the edge of my desk, eating a sucker.

"Oh, is that what you're mad about? The legalities of me seeing Ms. Belle without a nurse in the room?"

Duke is playing a dangerous game. One he might win.

"Or is it because you don't like to share Ms. Belle?"

Inhaling, I stride to my chair and throw myself down, cradling my head in my hands. "Fuck you."

"Fuck me? You mean, fuck Halle, right? Since she's the one suffering from your lack of OR time." He arches a brow, the humor disappearing from his tone. "Why won't you take her case, Brother?"

"You know why I can't," I say, breathing in and out, willing my hands not to shake at the thought of taking a scalpel to her skin.

"I know you can't keep doing consults. You have to let him go,

Vance. You're a surgeon. The best one in the state. Patients depend on you."

"Don't you think I know that?" I snap, dropping my hands. "Don't you think that's all I think about when I'm up pacing?"

Duke flinches. "I didn't mean for it to seem like you didn't care, but, dude, the longer you stay away from the OR, the more the anxiety will build. I've seen this happen to other surgeons. You can't let go of a lifetime of work. People make mistakes."

"Not me."

Duke smiles, but it's lacking. "Yes, Vance. Even you make mistakes. Lo—"

"Logan," I interrupt. "Logan, my best friend. Not just anyone."

Nodding, Duke continues, "Logan won't be the last case you botch."

That word. Botch. It sends a rush of panic through me, and I stuff my hands between my legs. "It will be if I never operate again."

"What's your plan then? Work as a professor at the university? News flash, Vance. You have a personality of a junkyard dog. Students would be terrified of you. Trust me, working in an OR—alone—is your best bet. You suck at peopling."

"What the hell is peopling?"

Duke shoves his sucker in my pen holder and stands. "It means get your ass back in the OR, where you belong, and help this girl. She moved across the country, just for the talent you want to piss away."

I stand. "You think I don't want to help her?" Blood rushes through my veins. "You think I like turning her away?"

"Don't you? I hear the rumors, big brother. You give this girl shit every day. She might as well be your personal dumping ground."

Holding my tongue, I grind down on my back teeth. The key to winning any argument with Duke is taking the fun out of it. If you don't give him something to run with, he'll tire of the conversation and move on to someone or something more entertaining.

"Fine. Have it your way." He makes for the door. "If you don't operate on her, I will. She's getting what she came for."

Fuck it. "You're not touching her." I'm in his face before either of us can process what I did.

"Oh, not only am I going to touch her, big brother. I'm going to perfect her for you. Maybe then you'll be able to tolerate her."

He's up against the door on his tiptoes before I realize it's me holding him there.

"Well, look who seems passionate about our new employee..."

I'm so sick of his games. "You know I can tolerate her," I grit, which only makes Duke laugh.

"I know. I also know that you want to do more than tolerate her."

"Our relationship is strictly professional."

"Then do her revision," he challenges. "Remain unaffected and perform the surgery."

Dropping his shirt, I let him go and step back. "Get out of my office, Duke."

And like the idiot he is, Duke takes a step forward, the humor gone from his voice. "I'll be in the OR with you." He puts his hand on my shoulder. "I won't let anything happen to her. I'll watch the monitors."

I shake my head. "Even if I could get past the shaking," I admit, "she wants *you* now."

He laughs, patting me like that's good news. "She'll come around. Trust me. Just be your charming self, and she'll be naked before you know it." He steps back and looks me in the eye. "Now, off I go to find myself a little afternoon snack. All this drama has me craving a sweet, submissive pussy."

I sigh but don't stop him as he leaves. He knows better than to let that snack be an employee. He's crazy but not stupid.

When he's disappeared down the hall, I close the door and drop back behind my desk, pulling up my calendar and finding room between all the consults for Ms. Aggravating and squeeze her in between two patients and add a note to the automated message.

*I can either carry you in or you can come willingly. Either way, I'll
see you at 2:00 pm.*

Dr. Potter.

Then I hit send. Ms. Belle is my patient, whether we like it or not.

The clock ticks, the soothing rhythm settling my nerves.

"Serena." I buzz my assistant.

"Yes, Dr. Potter?"

"Is my two o'clock ready?"

When Serena hesitates, I stand. I was serious about dragging Ms.
Belle in for this consult. "Never mind, Serena. I'll take care of it."

"Yes, sir."

At least someone does as they're told in this office.

Wrenching open my office door, I pound through the hallway,
pausing briefly when Serena points to the file room where I turn, slamming the door behind me. "I charge a thousand dollars an hour for my
time," I say to Halle's back.

She pauses briefly before sliding the file in her hand between the
others. "I bet your mama is really proud."

This woman incites a flaming rage to my temper. "Get your ass into
room five," I grit, all but growling.

Her voice is saccharine sweet when she returns, "No, thank you."

"Fine," I tell her, knowing good and damn well I'm breaking all
the rules I lecture Duke on. Never force or pressure patients. It's their
body, their decision.

But this is what Ms. Belle wanted, was it not? The whole reason she
came to Texas and got a job in my office. What did she tell me that day?
So she could get a discount and possibly put her surgery on layaway?

The absurdity of her thought process still confuses me.

"Ms. Belle, we discussed this. I will carry you—"

At my words, she flips around angrily, pointing her finger at me just as I did to her yesterday. "No, you will not carry me, Dr. Potter. You want to know why?"

I don't answer because anything I say right now will only upset her more. The fact is she has harassed me daily about this fucking surgery, even enlisting my brother to do it when I refused. She's getting a real consult this time, and nothing she's about to say will change that fact.

She sucks in a breath and moves forward but not close enough where I can grab her. "You won't carry me because I no longer want the surgery."

I rear back. "You don't?"

Her arms fold across her chest. "No, I don't. I've decided I can live with the scars." A quiver starts in her voice before I notice it taking root in her chin.

The crazy urge to go to her hits me square in the chest, but I tamp it down. I've broken enough rules for today. "Okay, if you're sure."

"I'm sure." She tips her chin up defiantly. It'd be cute if she wasn't about to cry.

I nod. "I'll tell Dr. Duke to take you off his schedule as well then."

"Fine," she snaps.

"Good," I return. "Glad that's settled."

"Can I get back to work now? Or would you like to harass me further?"

I grin. Even upset, she's all spitfire and brimstone.

"I'll come for you at five, Ms. Belle. I suggest you be ready."

And if she isn't ready… Well, I'd enjoy nothing more than another round of back-and-forth with Astor's pint-sized secretary.

"Did you run over someone's family pet this morning?"

"What?" I look over the top of my coffee, eyeing my brother who looks more disheveled than usual.

"Just wondering why you seem to be in such a good mood this morning."

Telling him that I'm looking forward to my first appointment would only start his morning off better, and considering it looks like he had a quickie in the elevator, I think he's had enough excitement for one morning.

"Can't I be in a good mood?"

Laughter explodes from Duke. "No, you can't. You're *never* in a good mood."

My eyes narrow. "Now you've resorted to lying."

"Tell me this, bro. When's the last time you remember smiling?"

That's easy. Yesterday, when I pissed off our new employee, but again, Duke doesn't need to know that. "I'm not even answering that absurd question. I smile, trust me."

Duke scratches his chin sarcastically. "You see, you might have sold me on that if I didn't live with you the first eighteen years of my life."

His persistence is starting to ruin my mood. "Again, I'm—"

Someone raps on the door before it's pushed open. "Dr. Potter, your nine o'clock is waiting in exam room one."

I stand. "Thank you, Serena. I'll be right in."

Forgetting Duke is still watching my every facial expression, I fail to school my reaction, and he doesn't miss it. "Ah, now I see. Shall I check the schedule and send the poor girl flowers? She must be in misery if she's making you happy."

"You won't say a word to her," I demand. "You've done enough."

Had it not been for him agreeing to do Halle's revision, I could have ignored her, but no, I could not stand back and allow him to perform a surgery he can't handle.

Uncrossing his legs, Duke sits up, a ridiculous expression on his face. "I see. Well, please let Ms. Belle know if she would like a consult on breast implants to let me know. We could probably do both—"

I'm in his face before I realize it. "She doesn't need enhancements."

My hands are shaking, and his gaze tracks the trembling at my side. "Agreed. But then again, I think we agree for two very different reasons."

I need to get out of here. Duke might enjoy seeing me squirm, but he's far too observant for my liking. "Get to work."

My demand only makes him laugh. "Yes, sir."

Shaking my head, I turn toward the door when he stops me.

"Hey, Vance?"

"What?"

"I'm serious about what I said."

I grip the door until my knuckles turn white.

"I'll be in the OR with you. I won't let anything happen to her."

CHAPTER TWELVE

Halle

A nineties playlist and a venti latte later, and I'm still pissed. Didn't I tell Vance that I no longer wanted the surgery? I'm pretty sure I did, and yet, he put me back on his calendar as soon as we arrived to work this morning. Without saying a word!

This man is allergic to not getting his way.

"Dr. Potter will want you to change into a gown."

I glare at Serena, who has been giving me the stink-eye since I walked in this morning. "Thank you, Serena. I'll consider Dr. Potter's wishes when he—"

The door opens, revealing the dark head of wavy hair and haunted eyes. "Ms. Belle. How are you feeling this morning?"

I'm feeling like God knew Vance would need to be hot because the personality he strapped him with will end up getting him junk-punched. Multiple times.

Before I flash him a fake smile, I address the second pain in my ass this morning. "That will be all, Serena."

I could swear Dr. Potter's mouth twitches.

"I don't answer to you," Serena snaps, her lips turning down into a pout that Dr. Potter ignores.

"It's okay, Serena," Vance soothes. "I'll be out in a moment."

More like he'll be out in a matter of seconds. This appointment will not take the allotted half hour he booked.

Serena huffs, giving me one last glare before she pulls the door closed behind her, leaving me and the beast alone. Hopefully, for the last time.

"Don't bother sitting," I say, still staring at the door. "You aren't staying. As I said yesterday, I no longer require your services."

Vance chuckles, and the sound snaps my head to where he perches on the exam table, one leg kicked up on the step. "I think that's the first time someone has ever told me," his voice lowers, and his eyes grow colder, "what to do in *my* exam room."

Okay, so maybe that wasn't the best way to start this conversation. "My apologies, but it seems like you need further instructions in this particular situation since you decided to make another appointment for me to tell you the exact thing I did yesterday. As you said, your time is expensive, and this appointment is a waste of those precious hours."

I hadn't planned to be such a shit, but this man needs someone to remind him that he is not the Messiah.

Rising, Vance sighs, a seductive smirk pulling up his lips. "Ms. Belle, what am I going to do with you?"

"Stop making me ridiculous appointments?" I suggest.

His steps are confident as he strides closer to where I'm standing by the sink. "You see, normally, I would agree with you, but unfortunately, it seems you're incapable of making sensible decisions on your own."

I snap, taking a step forward so I'm in his face. "You don't know me!"

He grabs my hand, wrapping it in his. When did I point at him?

"Don't I?" His brows rise. "Halle Elaine Belle, born December twenty-third in Cordele, Georgia."

I narrow my eyes and try pulling my hand free, but he doesn't let go. "You could have read that in my chart."

Like I didn't speak, his intense gaze steadies on mine. "You have a pet goldfish, who traveled here to Texas with you, only to move into a dump, six miles from my office." He pushes forward, pinning my arm to my chest. "What were your plans post-surgery, huh? Who's going to help you with recovery?"

I take a step back, the heat of his body feeling like second-degree burns. "I know it's hard for you to wrap your head around this, but some people take care of themselves. It's called being middle class."

His grin is sinister. "How were you going to change your dressings when you wouldn't even have been able to bend without crying in pain?"

I hold my chin higher. "Pain and I are good friends. We know how to tolerate each other."

"Doubtful."

I hate him.

"Well, you don't have to worry about how I will care for myself postoperatively since—listen close—I don't want the surgery anymore."

"You're lying."

"And you're an asshole."

I'm so over this day.

"That may be so, sweetheart, but at least I'm realistic. You moved to Texas for a consult with me, and you're getting what you came for."

My jaw clenches, but he doesn't notice since he can't seem to pull his furious eyes from mine.

"You can't go through a surgery of this magnitude and go home to a goldfish. I won't allow it. I'm responsible for your recovery just as much as I am the surgery."

I'm not sure if that's a personal responsibility or a customary one for surgeons, but I can't think straight with him this close. "Are you saying if I find someone to care for me, you'll do the surgery?"

Dammit, Halle! You just told him you didn't want the surgery. But let's be real, we all know I'm lying.

"Yes."

One word that will change my life.

He said yes.

I cock my head to the side. "What if I can't find anyone? My parents are older and can't leave the farm."

His watch beeps, and finally, he drops my hand and steps back. "Time's up. Tell Serena to schedule a follow-up, and we'll discuss further."

"And if I decide on another surgeon in Texas?" I prompt, my face heating with anger that he didn't answer my last question.

"No one else will take your case."

I suck in a breath as he leaves the room without a backward glance.

The bastard.

I know he had to have made some calls. I called twenty-five surgeons in the area, and all of them reported they weren't taking on new patients after I gave them my name.

Dr. Potter had to have done something. I'm not even surprised, honestly. What did I expect from a man wound so tight, he could wind a clock with his ass? He's always going to win. You don't get to be at the top of the food chain without learning how to crush the competition.

Now that Vance has decided he wants me as a patient, he's determined to eliminate any competition. And I don't know why this irks the hell out of me. I wanted Vance to be my surgeon, but now? I think I'd like to have more leverage so he doesn't think he's the only one who can fix a few scars.

No one should have that kind of power or ego.

Dr. Potter needs to be knocked down several notches, and personally, I'd like to be the one to do it.

"I thought Astor told you to go home?"

His rough voice drifts through the room, deep and low. Thankfully, it's not as scary sounding as it was earlier. Still, facing him mid-eye roll would likely not be beneficial in keeping his calm demeanor intact. "I finished filing the charts," I say, ignoring his question and continuing to pick up the gauze scattered across the floor.

"And in case you forgot, Astor told you to leave."

I see his mood didn't soften with his tone, which should have been warning enough, but I'm tired and so over his tantrum.

"And in case you don't look at your employees' timecards, I clocked out two hours ago."

Yeah, I'm doing this for free.

I brave a look at Vance and immediately regret the impulsive decision when I find his jaw clenched, eyes furious, and fists balled at his waist. Yeah, popping off when he's had a crappy day wasn't the best decision. It's too late to take it back now, though.

"Ms. Belle," he finally grits out, straightening to his impressive height, "if you don't get yourself out of my exam room in the next sixty seconds, you're fired."

His words are so simple—so concrete. Yet, I still don't heed their warning.

"You'd fire an employee for going above and beyond her duty to ensure her employer's schedule ran smoothly tomorrow? Call me crazy, but I expected the opposite reaction."

Did I think he would give me a sucker and a hug? No, not really. But a *thank you?* Yeah, I don't think those two words would have killed him to mutter.

A scoffing sound breaks his frozen stare. "I expect my employees to follow orders. Anything less than full compliance is grounds for termination."

"Is that why you have several vacancies?" I prompt. "Because no one offers you their full compliance?" Except for Serena. She's made it clear whatever Dr. Potter wants, she delivers. Such a butt kisser... probably literally.

A hint of a volatile smile briefly crosses his face. "Exactly. Twenty seconds." He glances at his watch as if he's actually timing me.

Whatever. He already agreed to the surgery, whether either of us are happy about it or not. "I'm not leaving until this room is cleaned," I promise, dropping his stormy gaze and getting back to the mess.

His voice is clipped when he grinds out, "Time's up."

I shrug, not bothering to look at him. His frustrated face is likely still the same. "I'll pack my things when I finish."

"You'll leave now," he demands, the words strained as he pushes them past his annoyance. "I'm ready to leave."

I sigh. This man and his moods. "Dr. Potter," I say with fake bravery, "I'll leave this room when you drag me out of it."

The exam room is so quiet that I think he walked out, but when I look up, I see him standing in the doorway, his eyes focused on me like if he could set me on fire, he would.

"Either drag me or help me, Dr. Potter. Those are your only two options."

Where I got the nerve, I have no idea, but something about this man sparks a defiance deep inside me that I thought I'd long since put behind me.

A long silence passes between us before I hear Vance's sigh as he lowers to his knees.

I turn back to the mess in front of me and fail at hiding my grin.

He caved.

Big, bad, and severely broody Dr. Potter actually did something he didn't want to.

"Ms. Belle," he rasps out quietly.

Raising my head, I answer, "Yes, Dr. Potter?"

His eyes are like burning embers, alight with hot rage. "Next time you disobey me, I'll take you up on your offer and drag you out of here."

I swallow, my grin falling flat when he warns, "I'm not the man to test."

Perhaps. But then again, maybe his attitude could use a little challenge. "So, you're saying there will be a next time?"

His lip twitches. "I'm saying next time I won't be so amenable to following policy."

Is it inappropriate that the lower half of my body clenched at his threat?

Grinning, I ignore the tingles swirling in my stomach. "All I'm hearing is, *'I'll see you tomorrow.'*"

Vance just stares at me, his blinks slow and methodical before he inhales, and clips out, "You have thirty minutes and then we're leaving."

CHAPTER THIRTEEN

Halle

"I'm hungry."

I turn in my seat and blink at the man who changes moods like he does socks.

"Okay," I drawl. "Do you need to come in for a snack?" I motion to the motel door in front of where Vance's car idles. "I have cheese puffs."

He's calmed down quite a bit from earlier in the exam room. I don't know what changed, but I'm not mad about it. I can handle cranky Vance and moody Vance, but hungry Vance is a new one.

"I don't want cheese puffs." He frowns like saying the words personally offended his tastebuds.

"Okay, rude." I put my hand on the handle, and the locks click into place—Vance's sign that he isn't finished speaking.

"I want dinner," he admits clinically and detached.

Again, I try the handle, still finding it locked. "Well, I hope you enjoy your dinner. I've heard good things about several of the restaurants near here." I flash him a smile. "I suppose I'll see you in the morning?"

This time I wiggle the handle, so he knows I'm ready to get out. Other people are hungry, too.

Dropping his head, Vance takes a deep breath before he looks up, leveling me with a look of resolve. "Would you like to try one of those restaurants with me?"

Oh. *Oh.*

"Umm..."

"We can go over your surgery since office hours seem to offend you."

"Office hours don't offend me," I snap. "You gave me an ultimatum. That offends me."

He pushes back in his seat as if this sort of conversation is easier for him to deal with. "And have you found someone to care for you postoperatively?"

The smugness on his face deserves to be smacked. He knew I wouldn't know anyone around here to care for me. It's his way of getting out of doing the surgery. But he won't win this battle. I can be just as savvy. "Actually, I have."

I watch as the smugness fades into something like panic. "Who?" His entire posture has gone rigid.

Yeah, roll that feeling of defeat around, Dr. Potter. Taste it. Smell it. And get fucking used to it.

"Who doesn't matter. Just as long as he's there to pick me up upon discharge, correct?"

That crazy sexy muscle in Vance's cheek twitches as he puts the car in gear, reversing out of the parking lot.

"What are you doing?" I nearly shout. "Let me out."

For a moment, I don't think he's going to answer me, but when the motel disappears in the rearview mirror, he finally grits out, "We're going to discuss it over dinner. I need alcohol."

"And a restraining order," I add, taking pleasure in the return scowl. "You're really getting too comfortable with this whole kidnapping thing."

I chuckle at my joke, but then he mutters, "You're no kid," and I go quiet. The way he said it sounded like he was mad this wasn't a mere kidnapping.

"And you're no criminal. Yet, here we are."

"Here we are," he repeats, a less than amused scoff behind his words.

I don't know what to make of Dr. Potter and our interactions, so I decide that I'm just going to sit back and let him work through whatever he needs to while we, apparently, get dinner. Well, that is, until he pulls up to the valet for a prestigious restaurant I'm so not into. I want good, greasy food, not steamed vegetables and attitude. "I don't want to eat here," I tell him.

He flashes me a bored look. "Too bad. Get out."

And he's back to being a jerk.

Too bad I know how to deal with him now. Folding my arms, I watch as he gets out of the car, the valet opening my door.

I don't get out.

The valet won't pull me out of the car, and in front of all these people, neither will Vance. I can't help the big, stupid grin on my face when Vance comes around to the passenger side, a nasty scowl on his face. "Get out."

"No, thank you. I'll just wait for you to finish your meal." I make a show of looking around. "I might walk around and see if I can find a McDonald's."

He takes a menacing step toward me, and the valet moves aside, allowing him. "You'll do nothing of the sort. We're having dinner here." He scrunches his face. "Not at McDonald's or anywhere that has a cartoon mascot."

Like a crazy person, I reach out and touch the corner of his frown. "Most men typically ask women where they prefer to go on dates," I muse. "The whole alpha, demanding thing went out of style years ago. Nowadays, women like to be equals."

This man has two settings, angry and broody, so I'm not surprised when he leans over me, his breath grazing my ear. To the valet, it looks like he's sweetly undoing my seat belt, and I think he is, but the words that slip from his breath are far from romantic. "If you don't get out of this car, the valet will have a vivid image of what it sounds like when you beg for my mercy."

I swallow, my throat bobbing, my skin tingling with his seductive threat.

"Do you want him to jerk off to the memory of your screams, Peach?" The seat belt slides between us, setting my sensitive skin on fire. Why? Why do his animalistic threats send delightful shivers throughout my body? I should be pissed that he's basically giving me another ultimatum, but I'm not. Instead of being angry, I'm hot and bothered. It's been four years since a man has been this close. Four years since I've even tolerated or wanted a man. And the one who finally makes my lady bits quiver, is the very man who is delaying my dreams and being an overall giant pain in my ass.

His finger drags along my cheek, barely grazing the skin as he tucks a strand of hair behind my ear. "Test me," he threatens. "I'd love to show you how I can handle you off the clock."

If I didn't know any better, I would say Dr. Potter, asshole extraordinaire, is just as pent-up as I am. Could it be he hasn't been with a woman in a while, either?

"What's it going to be, Ms. Belle? A calm dinner or tomorrow's front-page news? I'm sure you'd love to keep it right next to the precious article that delivered you to my clutches in the first place."

Have mercy.

He is absolutely frustrating in the sexiest of ways.

Turning into his shoulder, I whisper, "I'll eat here if you promise we can stop for dessert somewhere cheap."

Pausing, he absorbs my words.

"Unless you'd love another go at your fifteen minutes of fame." I smile into the stubble of his cheek, the scratchiness making me shudder. "I'm sure your pretty face will only bring more potential patients that you won't operate on. You're running out of excuses, Dr. Potter."

I'm not the only one who has something to lose here. As sexy as Vance is, he doesn't really want to draw attention to himself, even if he would love to toss me over his shoulder and make me squeal in front of the valet.

"Do we have a deal, Dr. Potter?" I prompt when he keeps silent, his lips hesitating at my neck as he considers my offer.

"Deal," he clips, his voice sounding like gravel as he drags his face against mine, his fingers grazing dangerously close to my center as he lifts up and meets my heated gaze. "Always negotiating," he says, a barely-there smile as he stands, straightening his suit jacket and extending his hand.

I was raised with manners, so I smile, avoiding the valet's gaze as I take Vance's hand. "I wouldn't have to negotiate if you were more agreeable."

He jerks me into his side, propelling us up the steps. "And I wouldn't have to keep enduring your terrible negotiations if you would learn how to take no for an answer."

"We'll have to agree to disagree." I shrug, but I don't think he notices since he's already giving the hostess his seating preference, which is a small table in the corner by a window overlooking the river.

"Wow, this is pretty."

He makes a noise in his throat as he pulls out my chair. "And to think we could have a view of a drive-through."

I refrain from rolling my eyes in such a fancy place. "I'm too underdressed to eat here," I try to explain. With the multiple chandeliers and white linens, I feel like I need a ballgown and a tiara.

"You look fine." He scoots my chair to the table and takes the empty chair across from me, picking up his menu and scanning. I follow suit, but I stop, leaning over the table and whispering, "There are no prices listed."

I'm no idiot. No prices mean it's so ridiculously priced that the establishment is too embarrassed to list it. "I can't afford a two-hundred-dollar burger," I add, just in case he doesn't get what I'm saying. He might be the fancy surgeon making a thousand dollars an appointment, but I'm the broke girl sleeping in a rathole so she can afford revision surgery.

He barely spares me a glance. The only way I know he heard me is the slight twitch of his lips. "They don't have burgers," he says unhelp-fully. "Or fries. You'll have to order something less *Happy Meal*."

Sucking in a breath, I control my temper. This is Vance's happy place. Rage and irritation are his catnip, and I refuse to feed his need. "What do you suggest then, Dr. Potter?" He cocks his head and pauses.

"I'm serious, what's good here? Surely, you have a preference."

The waiter appears before Vance can answer. He orders both of our meals—steak—adding a bourbon to his order and water to mine.

"Am I not allowed to have a drink?" I fold my arms across my chest, my mood tanking by the minute.

"Did you want a drink?" The way he asks me all-knowingly is enough to cause me to clench my fists so tight my nails leave marks in my skin.

"Well, no, but I would like to have been asked."

The waiter brings his drink out and sets it on a napkin in front of him. He picks it up, downs the whole thing, and hands it back to the server, ordering another. "Would you like a drink, Ms. Belle?"

I hate him, I really do. "No, Dr. Potter. It seems like one of us might need to stay sober, just in case this ends up with jail time." I smirk. "The jury will be more swayed with the sober testimony."

Vance's fists clench, his entire body rigid.

"It was a joke," I amend. "I don't want anything to drink. Perhaps next time, you could be polite and ask me, though." I offer him a grin as a peace offering. "Just in case I'm feeling frisky."

His eyes drift to the table, and he nods. "Of course."

And now, I feel like an asshole. Fortunately, the waiter comes back with his drink, and he quickly disposes of it like last time, barking for another.

"Should you be drinking so much before dinner?"

He seems a little more relaxed than a few minutes ago, which I can only attribute to the alcohol. "Shouldn't you be telling me about this new caregiver of yours?" He leans back in his chair, his body relaxed as he turns his attention to me.

"What's there to tell? He's available and can help me redress the wounds as needed." I shrug. He's not getting anything else. Well, I don't necessarily have anything else to say since, technically, said caregiver doesn't know he's going to be—or at least pretend to be—a caregiver.

Vance's jaw clenches. "This caregiver better not be the same one who inflicted these wounds in the first place."

I suck in a breath. "No," I finally say after a few minutes. "It's not him."

"Is he still in the picture?" His jaw is tight enough it could crack nuts.

"No. I haven't seen him since it happened."

Vance stares at me, angry and broody across the table. Neither of us is willing to say more as dinner is served, eaten, and cleared away. It isn't until we leave that things turn interesting.

CHAPTER FOURTEEN

Vance

I'm drunk. Terribly drunk. Asking her to dinner was my first mistake. Getting hard while arguing with her in the car, my second. My third came when I couldn't control the thoughts swirling through my head.

Juries.

Hit and runs.

Her beautiful body crushed under a tire.

The images in her file were like crime scene photos. This determined Georgia Peach, sweet and supple, crushed by a man and his anger. Yet, here she is, enduring blow after blow from me. All for a fresh start and refined scars, so that she's not reminded of her past.

But that's the problem for both of us. Nothing we do will ever change our past. It's shaped us—molded us into the people we've become. For her, she became more determined and passionate about her dreams. For me, I caved under the weight. I lost sight of the man before the tragedy. And yet, every day, I go into the office and lie to patients. I promise them hope I can't seem to deliver.

But I didn't want to do that to Halle.

When she came to my office, looking at me like I was the one who was going to change her world... I just couldn't put her through more pain. She'd suffered enough.

"Vance, wake up." I'm pushed into something cold and hard. "I need you to get in the car. Can you do that?"

I can vaguely make out her frown in the dark. "You're not driving my fuckin' car," I mumble out, incoherently.

The valet opens the door, and she ignores me, giving me a shove. "I sure am, and you're going to shut up while I do it."

My ass hits the seat as the restaurant starts spinning around us. "This car is worth—"

She cuts me off. "Yeah, yeah. More than I make in a lifetime. I'm sure it drives just as well as an old Ford." She leans over me, her smile a clear indication that she's enjoying my drunkenness. "Do you need me to help you buckle up, Big Texas?"

"That's a stupid nickname," I tell her, reaching for the seat belt and finding nothing.

Great, tomorrow is going to be real fun. *Good decision-making tonight, Vance.*

I try for the seat belt once more, and she stops me. "Let me."

If I were sober, I would adamantly refuse, but as of this moment, I doubt I could work the latch, so I lean back and savor the smell of her perfume as she reaches across me and secures the belt. "I kind of like you restrained, Dr. Potter," she muses, giving the belt a little tug.

"Cute." She has no idea the line she's toeing with such comments.

She chucks my chin. "Don't worry, Dr. Potter. I promise not to take advantage of you while you're in such an inebriated state."

Somehow, I keep my mouth shut and don't tell her that I wish she would. It's been over a year since I've been with a woman. After Logan, I fucked every woman I could—including Serena. I thought it would chase away the demons of what I'd done. My brother would be so pleased to know that the reason we have a no-fraternization policy is because of me, not him. Things were out of control—*I was out of* control. I needed to get a handle on my behavior and nip whatever idea was forming in Serena's head, hence the policy.

It was a dick move.

One I will never make again.

"All right, where to, boss?"

Halle adjusts my seat and rearview mirror, looking incredibly out of place.

"Let's just call an Uber. I can pick up my car tomorrow."

She waves me off. "Don't be silly. I can drive us. You know, us women can do more than bear children."

Sarcasm is basically the truth wrapped in humor. "Is that the vibe I give off? That I only think women are good for bearing children?" Not that the idea doesn't sound appealing. Halle's body, with her smooth curves, beckons to be made round with a child—preferably mine.

Fuck, I really am drunk. Having children with any woman has never crossed my mind. My patients are my primary concern. I don't have time for anyone else.

Halle chews on her bottom lip, and I struggle to stay focused. "No, I suppose not. It's just alpha men tend to have simplistic views of women's roles in society."

I think I arch a brow. "I don't recall ever saying such a thing." I'd like to ask her if that's what the dickbag who hit her with his truck said to her all the time, but I don't. When I brought him up earlier, she clammed up, and maybe it's because I've had a rough day or the fact that I'm shitfaced, but the last thing I want is to be alone with my thoughts. The irony is, the more Ms. Belle talks, the less crappy I feel.

It's a shame that her perception of me is less than admirable. I can be a nice guy when my entire life and career aren't crumbling before me.

"You're right," she admits. "You've never suggested women weren't equals. Guess my past is bleeding through." The corner of her lip tilts up into a smile. "Let's get you home, yeah?"

Leaning forward, I focus on the onboard screen and set the GPS to route us to my house.

"Thank you," she says softly, putting the car in drive.

I steel my nerves as she pulls out of the driveway and onto the road. "Not bad," I praise.

She side-eyes me, her hands never leaving the wheel. "Did you think I was going to crash as soon as I pulled out"

Okay, so I'm not doing myself any favors here. "Not exactly," I try to explain. "It's just…" I exhale and close my eyes, letting my head fall against the headrest. "I haven't been a passenger in years. I can't remember what it feels like not to drive."

There. She can do what she wants with that information.

"So, you're a control freak?"

"Freak is such a negative word," I tsk, keeping my eyes shut. It's easier this way. The world isn't spinning, and I don't have to look at Ms. Belle as she takes in the truth of who I actually am. Spoiler alert, it's not the man in the article she cares so much about.

"You're right. I'm sorry. Freak is a terrible word. I just meant that you like having control. In every aspect of your life?"

Maybe it's the alcohol talking, but I take her question to specifically mean in the bedroom. "Yes." I open my eyes and direct my gaze to where she has her lip pinned between her teeth. "Does that disappoint you?"

In my head, that came out differently. I meant that I fell into her alpha male stereotype again, but then she shakes her head ever so slightly.

Huh. So, Ms. Belle doesn't mind a little dominant alpha in the bedroom? Interesting.

Fifteen minutes later, we're pulling into my driveway, the alcohol settling around me in a blurry haze.

"Wow. This is classy," Halle muses. "You live here alone?"

I cut her a look that says, *do I look like I tolerate other people in my space*, and press the button above her head. "Park in the garage. Try not to hit the other cars."

"So sweet. I bet your bed stays warm at night with that kind of pillow talk."

She's darling. "I prefer my sheets cold and my women colder. Keeps all those pesky feelings from warming up."

"Charming."

"I try."

Blessedly, Halle parks in the four-car garage without scratching the car or any of the others. "Do you think you can make it up the stairs?" she asks, getting out.

"I'll be fine."

I stumble on the first step, but I manage to open the door without incident, holding it until I realize she isn't behind me but rather, still next to the car.

"I'm just going to call an Uber." She waves goodbye like that's happening.

"You're not getting in a stranger's car at this hour." I tip my chin toward the inside of the house.

"But we have to go to work tomorrow."

I let out a breath. *What the fuck are you doing, Vance?* "Exactly. We need sleep. I have a guest room. We'll stop by your place in the morning." Miraculously, I manage not to call it a motel.

"Oh, no. I couldn't. I'll be ok—"

I'm down the steps—which seem steeper than I remember—snatching the phone in her hand before heading back, throwing over my shoulder, "I have cheese puffs, too."

I don't wait for her to follow. She will. Without her phone, she can't call for a ride, and I don't live in an area where taxis frequent. The nearest neighbor is two miles away. Unless Halle wants to sleep out under the stars, she better follow me before I pass out.

I'm already pouring another drink when she finally comes in, her cheeks red and her brows furrowed. She's adorably pissed, and my dick stirs. "Give me back my phone."

I slide a gaze at the clenched fists at her side. "It's on the table. Believe it or not, I'm trying to be a gentleman." I flash her a wink. "Not a kidnapper."

"Ha. A gentleman would never take a lady's phone." She's all fire and brimstone, and I don't fight the smile when I take a sip of bourbon. "I never said I was good at being a gentleman."

"Isn't that the damn truth." She scrolls through her phone, presumably so she doesn't have to look at me.

"Do you want a drink?" It's the least I could do since she gave me a ride home without wrecking my car.

"No," she storms over, "and neither do you." Reaching for my glass, I hold it above her head, out of reach. "Vance. I'm serious. I think you've had enough."

Not quite. I'm still conscious, but I don't admit that out loud. It's best if Ms. Belle doesn't witness the monster coming out. Trust me, she needs me to drink a few more glasses.

When she realizes she's never going to reach the tumbler, she gives up with an annoyed huff. "You're going to be hungover for your consults tomorrow."

I empty the glass in one go and hiss. "It helps with lying to them."

My statement gives her pause. "You mean when you put them on your OR schedule?" Her voice quiets, and she looks down at the ground. "You're going to cancel them, aren't you?"

At first, I wonder how she knows I put them on my OR schedule, but then I remember that we all share the same OR schedule. Astor would have given her access to it. "Yes." I don't feel like lying.

"And you feel bad about it?"

"Yes."

She steps closer, looking up to meet my eyes. Damn, she's beautiful, with her golden hair fanned out past her shoulders, resting along her breasts. So soft. So resilient.

"So why not tell them no?"

I brush my fingers along her cheek. "Like I did with you?"

Her throat bobs. "Yes, like me."

"You're... different."

I'm not in the mood to swap tragic stories, so I offer her a pained smile and brush past her. "Follow me, I'll show you to the guest room."

CHAPTER FIFTEEN

Halle

Vance gives me ragey whiplash.

Why can't he just answer a simple question? What's so awful about my case that he wasn't willing to take a risk? It wasn't until Duke agreed to take me on that he agreed. I want to know why.

I've seen the cases Astor takes on. They're horrific. Those poor families. Sometimes, I think Astor can't possibly help them, then I hear him promising that he'll do the best he can. If Astor can take on cases that seem nearly impossible, you would think his superstar brother, who is known to take the high-risk cases, would be willing to take on a few scar revisions without batting those gorgeous eyelashes.

Vance stops and opens a door. "There's an en suite and fresh towels in the cabinet."

All I can do is nod as I take in the guest room that's twice the size of my current motel room. A king-size bed sits in the middle of the room with sheer, white curtains covering the wall-to-wall windows. "Thank you."

He nods and steps back. "I'll find you a T-shirt to sleep in."

"That's okay," I say distractedly as I admire the white, fluffy bedding that looks like something out of a magazine. "I can just…"

I turn around and he's gone.

Perfect. Now, what do I do? Wait? Disappear into the shower and let him creep in and leave the T-shirt on the bed?

I move into the room, locating the en suite easily. As I expected, it's larger than a normal-sized bathroom. I'd even wager it's ten times the size of the motel bathroom.

You know? I think I *will* disappear into the shower. The damn thing has a rain showerhead for goodness' sake. Do you know the last time I've been under a rain showerhead? Never, that's when. Don't think I'm too shy to take him up on the offer, either.

You only come to Texas once.

I don't remember falling asleep.

I remember thinking the shower was sent straight down from Heaven. It was skin-searing hot with the rain shower that felt like tiny fingers massaging the tension from my shoulders.

It. Was. Delightful.

More than delightful, really, but then I slipped the softest T-shirt— from Harvard, no less—over my body and climbed into a bed that must have been stuffed with fluffy clouds and baby smiles.

I was out before my head hit the pillow.

Unfortunately, I didn't stay that way.

My hips throbbed and my knee ached. I needed more than the four pillows on the bed. Like the bed, they were soft. Too soft for someone who needed to sleep with them between her legs to relieve the pressure. At home, I have a bed specially made for people who suffer from arthritis and joint problems. It's hard and feels a lot like a rock when you first lie down. But, it supports my body the way it needs.

Easing out of bed, I tiptoe into the kitchen. Without more pillows, I'll need a pain reliever. Otherwise, Vance will end up carrying me into work. I certainly can't have that. We've already crossed far too many lines tonight.

What was with the forced dinner and sleepover? It's like Vance tries to be nice but gets confused on how *nice* is supposed to go. But, I've long given up trying to figure out how he works.

I'm just grateful he didn't act like it killed him for me to stay. That must be progress, right? Maybe, if we can be friends or even tolerate each other, he'll still agree to the surgery when he hears I don't exactly have someone to take care of me afterward.

Like the bathroom cabinets, Vance's kitchen cabinets are empty of painkillers. I don't know whether to cry or pour myself a glass of bourbon. Alcohol only numbs the pain for a little while. After that, I feel worse. Tomorrow, I will feel like death with bad hips.

Ugh. Guess it's physical therapy stretches after all.

I honestly hate stretching. Part of the reason is because that's all I've been doing for years. It isn't relaxing yoga that you see on TV. It is gut-wrenchingly painful. It defines the term "pain before gain."

In order to move again, you need to stretch muscles that feel like they are ripping you in half. It's the shittiest solution to pain I've ever encountered.

But it works.

And that's how Vance found me on the rug of his living room, moaning and cursing with both feet in the air doing my best at the "happy baby pose."

"Halle?"

I can't even look; I stay frozen in place. Maybe he'll just feel weird and walk away. He tends to do that fairly often.

But then, I realize I don't have on any underwear. I took them off to shower, and I don't know about most women, but I'm not putting on dirty underwear once I'm clean.

I let my feet drop hard onto the floor, sending a shooting pain up my hips. "Oww," I cry, pulling down Vance's college shirt as far as I can, without ripping it from my shoulders.

"Are you okay?" His voice is much closer than it was before. So close, in fact, that if my eyes were open, I would swear Dr. Potter is right beside me.

I let out a groan. "Can you just go back to sleep and pretend this was all a dream?"

I'm pretty sure I've embarrassed myself enough around this man with all the begging and hatefulness. His seeing me commando, rolling around on his Italian rug, is too much.

"Open your eyes."

I notice the warmth of his hand first, hovering over mine, where it's still gripping the shirt, holding it to my knees.

"Just go back to bed, Dr. Potter. I didn't mean to wake you."

I wished he had just passed out from all the bourbon.

"You didn't."

Great. He's a night owl.

"I promise, I'm good. Just needed to stretch." It's like I can feel his gaze roving over my body, sharp and calculating. The doctor has awoken.

"Where's the pain?"

His hand presses down on mine, and I sigh. "Not to make this more awkward, but if you didn't already notice, I'm not wearing any underwear."

"I've seen vaginas before."

"Eww. Can you not say it like a doctor? It sounds weird."

He lets out a light chuckle. "And yet, you are my patient. Would you prefer I refer to your nether regions in slang?"

I nod. "Yes, please." No shame here. I don't need my physician to sound educated right now.

"Fine." His breath fans across my face. "I've seen pussy before, Ms. Belle. I assure you, I can remain professional."

The way he says pussy, all gravelly and low, makes me now want to hear him say it *un*professionally.

However, I'd prefer that time to be more when I'm not sprawled out in pain, my hoo-hah shining brighter than the moon, on my employer's living room floor. Yeah, I'd like a little more control of the situation and a lot less mortification.

"I appreciate the professionalism, Dr. Potter, but like I said, I'm fine." I force a grin, still squeezing my eyes closed. Immature? Sure. But I think we can all agree I should get a pass.

"I won't ask again," is his response. His annoying, bossy response. You'd think I'd be used to it by now, but I'm not.

I crack one eyelid open and find him staring down at me with a hard look on his face like he was ready to shake me. "Can you just find me a painkiller?" Seriously, maybe I can be a really bad girl and wash it down with alcohol, so I don't lie awake all night reliving this cluster-fuck of a night.

With a tilt of his head, not even anything that could be classified as a nod, Vance agrees. "After you tell me where it hurts."

And he just can't help but get his way. "Really, Vance?" I open both eyes so he can really see how annoyed I am with him right now. "Can you not just get me a fucking Tylenol?"

"Language," he scolds, covering my mouth with his hand. "Now, let's try this again. Where does it hurt?"

Maybe I was wrong about Dr. Potter. He's annoying as a regular person, but when he's in doctor mode, he's unbearable. What was I thinking wanting him as my surgeon? We'll kill each other before he finally gives me a surgery date.

He never moves his hand. It's not until I release my grip on the shirt and move his hand myself does he rock back on his heels, ready to listen. "My hips, okay?" I give him this look that says *are you happy now?*

"How much walking did you do today?" His gaze lingers at the hem of the shirt. I can tell he wants to look, but what could he possibly tell from examining my skin? It's not like a bone is sticking out.

But then again, now that I really follow his gaze—which travels up to my chest—I think maybe he wants to examine more than just my hips.

Snapping my fingers, I pull his gaze back to my face. "I didn't overdo it, if that's what you're asking. It's the bed. It's too soft, and you don't have firm pillows to support the right angle I need."

I realize a minute too late that my statement comes out sounding ungrateful. "Not that it's your problem. I appreciate the bed. It's the coziest one I've ever slept on. My body just hates me and likes for me to sleep on prison beds."

Vance pauses, likely deciphering the rushed explanation. "I have more pillows."

Okaaaay. "Great. If you can just help me off the floor and grab them, I will get out of your hair."

And be alone, where I can smother myself into one of those new pillows you give me.

"Let's finish stretching you out first."

Dear God.

My bare cooch just clenched hard enough to take my breath. This man—*the* Dr. Potter—just said a term I've heard said by multiple therapists a million times and never once did I get wet at them saying the words, *Let's get you stretched out.*

Heaven help me, the first thing that came to my mind was him stretching something between my hips, not my hips themselves.

Oh, Halle. Girl, you've got to find yourself a vibrator… like, yesterday. The no sex since Shithead is finally catching up to you. It's making you crazy.

"Halle?"

Vance's baritone pulls me back to reality—which is getting so much worse by the minute. "Yeah, uh, no." I shake my head. "I mean, no, thank you. It's a sweet offer, but I think I'm good. Just a couple pillows and a pain reliever, and I'll be on my way."

He sighs hard, but I don't let it bother me because I know how he likes to get his way.

But then he takes my calf in his hands…

CHAPTER SIXTEEN

Halle

"What are you doing?" I'm pretty sure I shouted the question.

Without pausing, Vance lifts my leg higher, opening my hips with a slight angle toward his chest. My shirt rides up my thighs, but I can't bear to look. The cool air is enough indication that I'm no longer covered.

Great, just freaking—ow, crap. "That hurts," I moan.

"That's because you don't drink enough water throughout the day." His voice sounds like velvet mixed with an ounce of arrogance. "And potassium."

"Thank you, Five-Food-Groups. I'll remember my banana and water tomorrow along with leisurely stretches by the water cooler."

Vance chuckles darkly, sounding like a sexy health demon. "You know, for someone who begged for my services, you sure don't take my advice."

"That's because your advice is smuuug—ahhh." His fingers knead the tight muscles in my calf, and it sends a shock of pain throughout my lower body.

"Deep breaths," he encourages, cradling my knee to his chest, the other hand drifting high on my thigh, dangerously close to my center. The tension and tightness seem to evaporate like a balloon releasing into the air as his fingers work the muscles there.

I drop back onto the floor, letting my head hit the plush rug. "Promise we'll never speak of this again?" I close my eyes, fighting the urge to look at his face since I'm literally dripping on his fancy rug.

How will I be able to look at him tomorrow after he's seen my pussy? Crap, he could be looking his fill right now and… I moan just thinking about Vance looking at my center. I'm locked between his chest and arm, spread open in his T-shirt. If only this opportunity came at a different place and time.

"Breathe, Halle," comes the whispered demand. "Open your eyes and look at me."

I appreciate that he's trying to be the professional in the room. I, on the other hand, am struggling not to envision his fingers slipping somewhere a little lower and much wetter.

"Just hurry," I whine, blowing out a breath. "I'm cold."

A total lie. I'm hornier than a teenager at prom.

"Almost done," he soothes.

Gah, even that sounds sexy.

He's going to find a wet spot on the rug. I just know it.

"Tell me about Georgia." Vance sets my foot on the ground.

I open my eyes just in time to see him move around to my feet. This time taking both of my ankles and pushing them toward my chest.

"Oh my gosh," I groan and cover my eyes. He has a prime view of all my lady bits. "Georgia is Georgia." I'm finding it hard to breathe, let alone concentrate while I can feel the heat of his stare at my core.

"What do you like about Georgia?" He pushes harder.

"Why?" I pant. "You thinking of taking a vacay?"

"Perhaps."

Perhaps. Such a snooty word. It's kind of hot, though. "Well," I grin, "should you ever decide to visit, North Georgia is exceptionally beautiful in the fall. And a lot cooler."

"Hmm…" He rolls my hips, bending my knees side to side, manipulating my hips until I'm languid and putty in his hands. "How's that feel?"

Like if I had balls, they'd be purple. But I'm pretty sure he means my hips, not my vagina. "Much better, thank you."

"Do you think you can stand?"

At this point, with all the adrenaline rushing through my veins, I think I could sprint from this room without so much as feeling my feet touch the ground. "Yeah," I admit, cracking open an eyelid and admiring the concerned frown on his face.

In this dim lighting, Vance looks even sexier with his rumpled bed hair and creased T-shirt. He doesn't look like the put-together surgeon in a crisp suit I've come to know and annoy.

At my staring, Vance arches a brow, waiting.

"Yes," I confirm, opening both eyes, "I can stand."

"You sure?" He doesn't seem convinced, and given all my moaning, I can see why. But I learned a long time ago that a pretty face and sweet gestures would never be enough to make me fall in love again. Lust? Maybe. But never love. Not again, anyway.

I promised myself that I would never hang my love on whispered promises. Actions. I need to see those promises in action before I ever drop my guard again. So, while Dr. Potter may be making my body hum under his fingers, my heart is still firmly locked away in ice, where it'll stay until I decide to let it defrost.

"Halle?"

I've gone silent, too busy reliving the past and not paying attention to the present. "I'm fine," I answer absently, almost forgetting Vance asked if I was okay to stand.

Suddenly, strong arms slip under my back and legs, lifting me. "Wait!" I scramble to hold on to something, but I can only lean into the aggravating man, cradling me to his chest. I wrap my arms around his neck, which smells pretty freaking amazing if I must admit.

"I told you I could stand," I grumble as Vance walks us back into the kitchen.

"Not fast enough." He nods to the refrigerator. "Grab two waters."

Tilting my head back, I meet Mr. Impatient's eyes, and yep, he's serious. "Okay," I agree. "Put me down and I will." Dr. Potter has a nasty habit of just picking me up and moving me to the location he prefers. It's a serious problem he needs to address before it gets more out of hand.

"Vance?" I try, when he just stands there, his grip even tighter than before. "I'm serious. Put me down."

He blinks slowly as if I didn't speak. I swear he could drive a nun to drink with his stubbornness.

"So, we're really doing this?" I motion the few inches between our chests.

"Seems like it's the only way you follow directions," he finally says, smugness creeping into his tone.

This man needs a serious reality check.

I fold my arms and lean back into his arms. Never mind that I really would love a pain reliever and sleep, this lesson is much too important for Vance to miss. Sometimes, people can't just be moved until they do what you want.

Vance shifts his weight in response. "You can either grab a bottled water or you can drink from the bathroom sink. Your choice."

How sweet.

And annoying.

"Fine, but this little showdown is not over."

He nods in agreement like he's looking forward to our next run-in and shifts so I can open the fridge, grabbing two bottles.

"The only reason I'm doing what you want is because I don't want to deal with a moody *and* sleep-deprived Dr. Potter tomorrow."

"Good thinking."

He doesn't even deny the fact that he's intolerable on workdays. He simply walks us down the hall and past...

"Where are you going?"

He passes the guest room and proceeds down the hall where I'm starting to think his room is.

"Vance? Are you really not going to answer?"

He kicks a bedroom door open farther, revealing a room that reeks of masculinity and wealth. Gray walls, minimal furniture, and a bed made for a king. The massive California-king sits in the middle of the room, imposing and... destroyed. The black satin sheets look as if Vance spent the evening wrestling instead of sleeping and are mostly on the floor while the pillows are scattered about the mattress.

"What'd you do in here?"

He lowers me to the bed, the mattress firm, the sheets cool against my skin. "Slept."

I think his Harvard education failed him. "Sleeping is usually peaceful."

Those dark brows of his arch. "Is that why I found you on the floor of my living room? All the peace in the guest room got to be too much?"

"I'm disappointed in you, Dr. Potter. Sarcasm is such cheap humor. I thought it would be beneath you."

I didn't really. Sarcasm seems right up Dr. Broody's alley. With his arrogance and fine clothes, it only seems fitting that his humor would be sarcastic. Besides, how else would he communicate with us regular people?

Leaning back against the leather headboard, I make myself comfortable in sheets that smell earthy and rich, just like Dr. Potter. Vance's bed, as much as I hate to admit it, feels great. Firm and supportive, just how I like my mattresses and, coincidentally, my men.

Opening the closet, he pulls two pillows down from the top shelf and tosses them onto the bed. "Go to sleep, Halle." No emotion. No hint of a smile. Just an order like the good doctor is used to giving.

Taking one of the pillows, I pull it to my chest like a shield. "Where are you sleeping?"

Vance disappears into the bathroom, not bothering to answer (like usual), and returns with a blue pill in his hand. "Here, take this. It'll help with the pain and inflammation."

Seeing how this blasted pill was what started this whole mess, I take it from his hand without argument and swallow it dry. "Thank you."

I let the sincerity of my words linger between us. Not that I imagined Vance would be an asshole while I was in pain, but I didn't expect the gentle but firm way he's cared for me tonight. He didn't have to help me stretch or offer me his firmer bed. Honestly, I would've been okay with a Tylenol and an Uber.

"Roll over."

My eyes widen at the roughness of Vance's clipped tone. "I'm sorry?"

With a firm hand, Vance presses down on my shoulder, tugging the pillow from my arms. "Look, I appreciate your kindness tonight, and while I think you're pretty hot, I think it would be inappropriate for us to sleep together as a thank you."

Pausing, I swear Vance fights off a smirk, but it's gone before I can be sure. "While I'm flattered you think I'm hot, Ms. Belle, I don't sleep with employees or patients." He pushes harder and I go down to the mattress, feeling heat rising into my cheeks.

"Roll over." This time, he doesn't wait on me. He gently rolls me toward the door, facing away from him. If there was a time I wanted to burrow under the covers and hide, it would be now. Vance was just trying to make me comfortable, and I basically told him I thought he was hot. At least I said I didn't want to sleep with him, right?

I don't know why his dismissal stings, but I'm hoping it's because I'm tired from this weird night.

"I..." Vance clears his throat, and for a second, I think he's going to apologize. But then, his hands are on the back of my thighs. "I need you to open your legs." He pushes my knees at an angle and slips his fingers between my thighs, gently lifting, the cool air reminding me that I'm indeed still pantyless.

"I can take it from here." Reaching back, the hand not between my legs stops me.

"Spread your legs for me, Halle."

It's like he flipped a switch. My body heats from his words, tingles starting in my toes and racing upwards where wetness pools between my legs as his body bears down on me, holding me in place.

Don't groan, Halle. You'll only make this situation more awkward.

Inhaling, I try relaxing. No one needs to know that Dr. Potter's words have made me wetter than I've been in years. Before Shitbag. Before the accident. I haven't been touched—cared for—in years. Hell, I haven't even wanted a man's touch since the accident.

And here I am, the surgeon—who unwittingly got me through the roughest years—with his hands on my body, asking me to open my legs for him. Granted, he's trying to alleviate the pressure on my hips, but tell that to my body.

All I can feel is him and the reaction I have to his touch as he slips a pillow between my legs, his fingers accidentally grazing my core, pulling a moan from me.

"Oh, fuck," I moan, gripping the sheets and burying my face in the mattress. Maybe I can just die, and he'll let me.

"I'm sorry." His voice is thick and raspy. "I didn't mean to—"

Involuntarily, my legs tighten around the pillow, trapping his hand between them. "Oh, no." I shove my face further into the mattress. "Please just go." I'm begging, and I don't even care. If I never see Dr. Potter again, it'll be too soon.

My body, clearly, cannot be around him without losing its mind. I don't know how it'll work if he actually goes through with the operation. Thankfully, I don't have anyone to help me recover, so I can save that worry for another day. Tonight, I just need him to remove his magic hands and delicious smelling body from my vicinity.

"Are you still in pain?" His hand slips gently from my legs.

"No," I groan. "Just go."

Not surprisingly, he doesn't, his hands smooth down my hip to my ankle, gently lifting and easing another pillow between them. "Better?"

I can't respond. If I do, something crazy embarrassing will come out, and my soul can't take much more humiliation in front of this man.

"I'll take that as a yes." The man behind me chuckles.

I want to smack him, but then I might just come if I put my hands on him.

"Goodnight, Halle." With that parting whisper, Dr. Potter pulls the sheet over me and walks out, leaving me to alleviate a whole different kind of tension in his bed.

CHAPTER SEVENTEEN

Vance

I can still smell her on my fingers.

And that wouldn't have been a problem if I hadn't been surrounded by her scent. Tropical, sweet, succulent. The smell of her shampoo drove me fucking crazy all night as I lay on the guest bed, surrounded by the thoughts of her pussy. Soft, wet. The imagery of her lying on my rug, completely at my mercy as I worked the tightness from her body.

Her moans still linger in my head as I grip my cock in my hand, tugging harshly as the cold water pounds onto my back. All I see is the open space between her legs. Perfect. Sweet. Scarred. Strong.

Dropping my head to the tile, I yank brutally. I can't rid myself of the feel of the soft skin between her thighs coated with her need. I can't allow myself to get involved with a patient, especially not with Ms. Belle. I've already destroyed one patient. I refuse to destroy another.

My brothers don't deserve to lose the practice they worked hard to build.

Their patients deserve to keep their services.

So, while I'd like nothing more than to bury my bad days in Ms. Belle's pussy, I can't. Astor and Duke deserve my full attention. And my attention belongs in the office with my patients and my ten o'clock meeting.

Increasing my speed, I tug harder and faster, ridding the image of Halle beneath me, wet and supple. I can't be responsible for more. She needs a physician, not a one-night stand. After what she's been through, she deserves someone who's worthy.

I am not that man.

A heaviness fills me, and I give my cock one final pull, emptying out onto the tile with a shout. Ms. Belle is my employee. My patient. We are not friends. It's best she understands that last night was a mistake. It won't happen again. I'll make sure of it.

"Can I borrow your charger?"

My gaze drifts from my tie to the mirror. Halle is still in my college T-shirt. My dick thickens at the sight. "You should change."

"And you should learn some manners." A smirk plays on her lips, which doesn't help matters.

"I need to leave for the office soon." *Professional, Vance. Keep things professional.*

"Same. That's why I need a charger." She takes a step around me, slipping between me and the mirror, taking hold of my tie. "I need to call for a ride. I can't show up in the same clothes from yesterday."

That's for fucking certain.

"I'll give you a ride home." It's the least I can do before going back to being a dick to her.

She loops my tie around, her hand grazing mine. Memories of last night come rushing back. I drop my arms to my side and try stepping back, but she has a grip on my tie, holding me still. Holding my breath, refusing to breathe her in, I meet her gaze full of amusement. "Sucks, doesn't it?" She threads the tie, tugging it through the opening. "Being at someone's mercy?"

I swallow, releasing a breath as she pushes up against me. "Though, I can understand the appeal." She flashes me this adorable wink. "Power trip, right?"

She has no idea. "I don't know what you mean," I lie, but she doesn't fall for it.

"Of course." She yanks on the tie, and I catch myself before coming chest to chest with her. "I need your charger, Dr. Potter."

I snatch the tie from her hand and take a step back. "Get dressed, Ms. Belle, or you'll go to the office in my shirt." I walk backward to the door, ignoring the words, *keep it professional,* swirling through my head. "We have Italian rugs there as well."

If she would have been closer to my dresser, she would have thrown something at me. Instead, she merely grits her teeth, flashing me a harsh smile. "As you wish, sir."

I gave her fifteen minutes before I ordered her into the car. She didn't speak to me until we pulled up to Clyde's Motel. "You're going to be late." She looks at me, confused.

"My first patient isn't until ten."

I haven't always been a bastard.

She eyes the door to her room.

"I have some calls to make. I'll wait for you out here."

"Out here?" Her eyes look like giant sapphires as she just stares at me.

"Yes, out here." Those plump lips of hers start to twitch, and I add, "Hurry before I lose my patience." I seriously need a punch to the face.

Halle chuckles out this dainty laugh and reaches for the door. "Sure thing, Vance."

"It's Dr. Potter, not Va—" She slams the door, cutting me off and inciting fury in my bones. Maybe it's that southern accent or the playfulness in her tone, but she irks me to the point of madness. I need another sparring round with Astor. Maybe he can beat out whatever this is.

When Halle has disappeared into her room, I pull out my phone and dial Richard. He answers on the third ring. "I expected you to call yesterday when I left you a message."

"And I expected you to make an appointment to speak with me like everyone else."

It's been a rough twenty-four hours, and unfortunately, Richard will bear the brunt of my frustration. Again.

"I'm not everyone else, Dr. Potter. I'm your attorney."

And a really sucky one at that.

I sigh, getting out of the car. I need fresh air for this conversation. "What did you need?"

Richard pauses, likely deciding if he has the patience to deal with my shit through this entire case. "Calista's attorney set a deposition date."

"When?" I ignore the ringing in my ears, choosing to focus on the chipping paint on Halle's door.

"September."

Great. Only two months away.

I can hear the hesitation in Richard's voice before he adds, "This is important, Vance. If this deposition goes bad, you could lose your case."

And the practice.

Calista's lawsuit is personal, but she's attacking my practice and therefore, my patients. They don't deserve to be without access to plastic surgeons. We're the only practice left in the Bloomfield area. The other plastic surgery office closed last year.

"I understand, Richard." Gritting my teeth, I pace around the parking lot as Richard rambles on about proof and experts. I don't absorb any of it. All I can see is his face, begging me for help.

"Please, Vance. I trust you with my life." Dark circles framed his eyes. *I'd never seen him so haggard. Then again, I'd never seen him beg, either. "Please, brother. Don't let me lose her."*

"Vance? You still there?" Richard's clipped words pull me from the memory—the never-ending nightmare that always ends with me drunk, surrounded by broken glass.

"I need to go." I swallow past the knot in my throat.

"We need to prepare for your deposition."

No matter how many hours I pay Richard to prep me, the story is still the same. "Have Serena put it on my calendar."

"Dr. Potter, I know Logan was your—"

I end the call. Richard is paid by the hour, and that sentence was headed in the direction of fatherly advice—which he can keep. I know what I did, and I'll live with the consequences.

"Halle!" I bang on Ms. Belle's door. I don't know how long she needs to get dressed, but she knows I'm in no mood to wait much longer.

"Chill, asshole. She'll be out in a minute."

The smoke and asshole comment I could ignore. But it's the "she'll be out in a minute" that has me staring down at a five-year-old in two seconds flat. "How do you know Ms. Belle?"

"Ms. Belle?" The teenager cocks a brow, a fuck-all grin aimed in my direction as he exhales smoke onto my suit. "Is that what you call her?"

I narrow a gaze at the prick leaning back on two legs in a plastic chair. "What do you call her?"

He tsks. "That's not how we play this game."

I'm going to jail today, I can feel it. First, Halle pushes me with the whole tie thing. Then, Richard shits on my mood with a deposition date. Now, this fucking kid thinks he's going to intimidate me with cryptic conversation. Yeah, not happening.

I take a step closer and tower over the boy, who, likely, is only a few inches shorter than me, and snatch the cigarette from his mouth.

"Hey!"

I kick the legs of his chair and toss the cigarette, grabbing him by the shirt and hauling him against the door before he even realizes what happened. "I better not even catch you thinking about the woman in that room, you little perv."

"Ahh, I see." His fucking grin pisses me off. "You're—"

"Dr. Potter!"

I drop the teenager as if he were on fire and step back, his laughter filling the silence as I stare at Halle's wide eyes and frown.

"What are you doing?"

She rushes over to the teenager, who waves her off, already putting another cigarette in his mouth.

"I'm fine." The boy dusts himself off and flashes me a grin before addressing Halle, who is fretting over the plastic chair—that I broke. "Don't worry about it, Hal. I'll steal another one from next door."

Hal?

That's what he calls her? Hal.

I chance a look at Halle. Surely, she can't like that ridiculous pet name.

"You sure?" She seems concerned more with the chair than she does with the ridiculous pet name.

"Positive. Go before you're late for work." He plucks the chair from her fingers and winks at me. Blood pounds in my ears, and I find myself stepping forward.

"What is wrong with you?" Halle appears through the haze of red and shoves me back a step. "He's just a kid!"

Legally, he might be, but the hate-glare he shoots me tells me this kid has seen more than most adults have in a lifetime. This is a man in a teenager's body. And he's my employee's neighbor.

"Let's go." I grab Halle by the arm and pull her to the car as she protests, spouting off some shit about being rude. I couldn't care less how her hormonal neighbor feels about my manners. Frankly, I don't care what she thinks, either. All I think about is getting the fuck out of here and drowning myself in a glass of bourbon for the next eight hours while seeing patients that I won't treat and lying to my brothers that I'm resuming surgeries.

Life is fucking peachy.

"Get in the car, Ms. Belle, or I'll show junior here how well you behave under my hands."

She jerks to a halt, her eyes narrowing. "I don't know what your fucking problem is this morning, Dr. Potter, but I hope you shove it where the sun doesn't shine."

She wounds me with her harsh insults.

"Get in the car." I take a step forward. I'm done playing with her today.

Hell, I'm done with everything.

I made a mistake by bringing Halle back to my place. It's not my fault she won't take my offer and see another surgeon. I'm not responsible for what happens to her here while she waits on me to perform her surgery.

Which I won't because there is no way I'm discharging her back to the fleabag hotel with a horny teenager to check on her.

She needs to go home.

And somehow, I need to convince her.

CHAPTER EIGHTEEN

Halle

It's fine.

Everything is seriously *fine*.

Astor just needs me to bring a box of pamphlets he forgot...
to *Napa*!

I've never been on a plane. Heck, I don't even know how to get to
the airport. And to set up the private jet to escort me to Napa? Yeah,
that'd be an OMG. What was I thinking taking a job as his secretary?

I was thinking Dr. Potter would have agreed to do the surgery by
now, and I'd be in Hollywood, living out my newfound freedom as an
actress. But that hasn't been the case at all.

Duke. I need Duke. He'll know how to set up the jet and perhaps
prescribe something to get me through the plane ride. Since I found
Vance with my neighbor's shirt in his fist, he hasn't spoken to me. His
silence probably has nothing to do with my neighbor and everything to
do with the night we spent together. The night when his hand felt the
wetness between my legs.

Honestly, it won't hurt my feelings if he blocks the whole night out. I did.

Okay, I'm lying. I relive that night on the daily. When I can't get comfortable on the motel mattress, I envision Dr. Potter sliding a pillow between my thighs, the earthy scent of his sheets filling my senses as his fingers fill another sensitive part of me.

Shit. Napa.

Jumping up, I shake off the flush and nearly sprint to Duke's office, where I'm met with an empty desk, but not an empty office.

"Duke's in surgery," says the man who haunts my daydreams, pulling his gaze from a chart to address me. "Did you need something?"

I swallow. This is not something I want to admit to Dr. Potter. He's liable to fire me on the spot for being unable to fulfill my job duties. "No, that's okay." I offer what I hope is a sweet smile. "Thank you, though."

I turn to leave when his raspy voice stops me. "Peach."

Peach.

He called me Peach again, not Ms. Belle. Not even Halle. He went with Peach.

My mouth sticks, and I'm barely able to get out the squeaky, "Uh-huh?"

Those eyes, the color of an emerald, assess me with scrutiny before deciding he needs a closer look. He drops the file on the desk and comes around, standing in front of me, his fingers taking a piece of hair and tucking it back behind my ear. "What's wrong?"

Well, we could start with the obvious. Dr. Potter is touching me and not in a doctor-patient way.

"Ms. Belle, I asked you a question."

Ah, there's the boss voice. Okay, things are right again in the world. Dr. Potter isn't losing his touch.

His hands go to my upper arms, and he gives me a small shake. "Answer me, dammit."

Is he concerned? Surely not.

"Five, four—"

My eyes go wide. "Are you counting down like I'm some sort of toddler?"

Vance visibly relaxes as his grip on my arms loosens. "No, I was counting to keep me from losing my temper." He shrugs, and it's absolutely adorable. "My therapist insists it works."

I flash him a smile. "Did it work just now?"

He drops his hands and exhales. "No. I still want to shake you."

"Why?"

His words are so matter-of-fact. "I know everything about everyone in this office... except you."

"You know more about me than most," I counter. After all, he has my entire history in a manila file in his office, not to mention he's had a close encounter with my lady bits.

"Well, all I know right now is that you look peaked and nervous in Duke's office." He tugs at his tie, giving it a nice yank. "And it's distracting."

Please.

I roll my eyes. "My apologies for the distraction, Dr. Potter. I simply needed Duke's help, but no worries, I can manage without him."

I step back, turning for the door. Surely, Serena can come down from her twat throne and help me with scheduling a flight? But then I remember this morning's coffee incident and reconsider. Dr. Potter seems amenable today. Perhaps he wouldn't fire me over a simple lack of knowledge. Astor never used the jet before, so it's not like I would know how to schedule a flight on my own.

But more importantly... "I need a sedative," I blurt out, enjoying the shock that passes over Vance's face.

"I'm sorry. Come again?" He's adorable when he loses his grip on control.

"I said, I need a sedative." Sighing, I wring my hands as I explain. "Astor asked me to bring a box of pamphlets to him in Napa." I wave my hands between us. "You know he's at the plastic surgeon's conference, and he forgot the pamphlets. He wants me to bring them to him in the company jet, but I don't know how to set it up, nor have I ever flown." I take a breath. "I can ask Serena about the scheduling, but that won't get rid of the nausea currently going on in here." I motion to my stomach, just in case he needs a visual.

Vance watches me intently, his gaze narrowed on my face. "You're nervous about the plane?" he asks slowly, like I may break if he speaks too quickly.

"I'm nervous about flying in general," I admit with a shrug.

Continuing to stare, Vance watches me carefully before stepping behind me. Closing the door, he leans back against it, giving me all of his attention while worrying that expensive tie between his fingers once more. "You've never flown before?"

At least he doesn't sound shocked.

"No," I explain. "Not since the accident. But even then, it was a helicopter, and I was sedated." I don't go into detail about how flying takes me back to the day I nearly died. When my entire life changed in an instant.

"I forgot the Georgia girl doesn't travel." Dr. Potter's voice interrupts my spiral into memories best left alone.

"She doesn't." I offer him a small smile. "That's why she needs a sedative, so she doesn't vomit all over the pamphlets when she finally figures out how to schedule the jet."

He's still examining me so closely, I think he's not going to answer me, but then he comes through as usual. Rude. "I'm not prescribing you a sedative."

I really should have known. I don't know why I even bothered explaining the situation to him. "Okay, thanks anyway." I try to keep the disappointment from my words and reach for the door handle.

He doesn't move. He simply stays put, watching me curiously. "What time does he need you in Napa?"

My heart speeds up. "Four."

Finally, Vance pushes off the door, his masculine scent of leather leaving me a little lightheaded. "I'll have Serena schedule the flight, and I'll meet you in my office in two hours," he says, opening the door for me.

"Two hours?"

His eyebrows rise. "Two. Don't be late."

"But…" What's happening here?

"But what?" Dr. Potter is back to his hateful self again.

"What if I throw up on you?"

He chuckles, guiding me out the door with a hand on the small of my back. "You won't."

He sounds so sure. "You decided to give me a sedative after all?"

"No." His eyes harden. "You're going to see the West Coast completely sober."

"With you?" Surely there's alcohol on the plane. I'm thinking he means sober in more of a medicated way.

His jaw tightens like he's suddenly realizing what he got himself into. "See you in two hours, Ms. Belle."

Dr. Potter's office door is cracked when I rap lightly. "Dr. Potter? Are you in here?" I call, pushing the door open.

There, spread out over a manila file are curls. Lots and lots of dark curls. Connected to those soft curls, is a man who'd fire me if he caught me staring at him while he slept with a full glass of bourbon clutched in his hand.

"Vance," I say gently, giving his shoulder a soft shake.

Dr. Potter's head snaps up quickly, his eyes fluttering open as he blinks at me sleepily before taking a look around the office. "Fuck," he mutters, rubbing at his face to wake himself up a little more.

"It's 11:30," I tell him as I sit down across from him. "You said you wanted me back here in two hours." I shrug, smiling. "I'm guessing you aren't ready to go?"

Didn't he say for me not to be late? And yet, here he is, not ready like he barked for me to be. I can't help the dumb grin when he groans and lets his head hit the desk in frustration.

Yeah, I caught Mr. Perfect Employer sleeping on the job. "I can take your bourbon instead of you if you'd like. That way you can stay here and nap. It would solve my problem and yours."

Seriously, he does look tired. I don't think I noticed earlier. Well, I didn't notice much probably because I was in such a panic. After Vance barked out his orders, I went back to my office, found the pamphlets, and raided the snack machine, then I felt better.

Vance might be bossy as a mother trucker, but he took care of me, even if he didn't want to. And considering all he's been doing is patient consults, he probably needed something else to do with his time. But it shocks me to find him asleep in his office.

"Do you need to stop by your place and grab your bag?" He completely ignores my comment about taking the bourbon instead of him. "I don't know if Astor told you, but the conference lasts all weekend. But since socializing is the least of my favorite activities, we'll leave Saturday."

"What the heck? Really?"

Vance's brows rise. "Don't tell me you have epic plans at Clyde's?"

I knew him calling my motel room, my place, was a one-off. "Actually, I do have plans. Thank you very much."

He grabs a few things from his drawer, a smirk playing on his face. "Oh, yeah? What kind of plans does one have with a goldfish?"

I hate him. I really hate him. "You know," I say, kicking my feet up on his desk for the hell of it. "Sometimes, I think you just like pissing people off. Keeps them from asking too many questions, I suppose."

He shrugs one shoulder. "I like staying focused."

"And what would that focus be since from what I see, you're only doing patient consults? Still."

The way I know I hit a nerve is by watching that glorious muscle in his jaw tick away. "Money. You wouldn't know anything about that, though."

I've been around Vance so much lately that his comment doesn't even sting. "You're right. I find that money corrupts even the best of men."

"Where are the pamphlets?" The hardness of his words clearly indicates that this conversation is over.

"By the door. The box was heavy, so I—"

"It was heavy?"

Vance's gaze turns harsh as he rounds the desk, bending down to get in my face so that when I speak, my breath fans along his lips. "Yes, but I was going to ask Serena if I could use the cart in the file room."

I watch as Vance breathes through his parted lips, noting the grip he has on the chair, caging me in. "And did she let you use it?" He finally grits out.

"I couldn't find her." I feel like I'm about to get bent over the desk and spanked, which… isn't as scary sounding as it should be.

"You shouldn't be lifting heavy boxes." His words are tight and clipped. How does someone just wake up pissed?

I pat one of his hands on the armrest. "Well, I don't want to be fired, either." I flash him a conniving smile. "Still got a thousand left before I'm fully funded for my surgery." I don't mention the caretaker piece since Vance's gaze hardens, settling on my hand.

"I don't want to see you carrying another heavy box."

"Technically, you didn't see me carry this one, so…"

It was the wrong thing to say. I realized it a minute too late.

CHAPTER NINETEEN

Vance

I hauled her out of the chair so quickly she didn't have time to react, let alone make another snarky fucking comment. "Get your shit. Now."

Grabbing my keys and phone, I snatch up the box outside my door one-handed. "Do I need to repeat myself?"

She stands next to my chair, frozen, and I think she might actually try mouthing off again. But with one unreturned smile, she quickly realizes I'm in no mood to play her games. This is why I can't do her surgery. Patients like her won't listen. She won't follow my orders, and I refuse to be responsible for her botched recovery.

And so far, I've been unable to convince her to leave.

It's terribly inconvenient.

Rudeness doesn't faze her, neither does ignoring her. Halle still shows up every day without fault. Astor has the model fucking employee. One who is stubborn and loud with her pastel work attire and paper bag lunch.

She's a real pain in my ass, which is not news.

I didn't expect to get to know Halle while she waits on me to pull my head out of my ass. Which is looking like never. Even if Halle found an acceptable caretaker to help her, I'm no closer to stepping back into the operating room than I was a year ago when this all started.

Halle and I are fighting against the current. Eventually, we'll drown.

After what seems like an hour-long stare down, Halle saunters past me, eyeing the handle of box clutched in my hand. "Seems like you shouldn't be carrying a box, either. You could hurt your hand."

And now she's just getting on my damn nerves. "Walk."

"Where to, sir?"

She fucking curtseys in the hallway. I can feel the growl rumbling through my chest. This woman was put on the planet to test me. "To the garage."

With a grin, she turns around and walks. "Sounds kind of dirty when you say it all rough like that. *To the garage where I will ravage you for all to see.*" She deepens her voice on the last part, which, I assume, is to imitate me. She sounds ridiculous.

"How professional. I can see why my brother hired you."

"He hired me because I'm immune to Duke's charm." Her brows do this weird jumping thing.

"Is it too late to take the bourbon offer?"

I sigh, and she whips around, a wide smile spread across her face. "Did you just make a joke?"

"No. Can you please hurry? I'd like to leave before dark."

"Oh, right." Her face frowns. "Are you sure I need a bag?"

"Are you sure you really have plans?"

She exhales and looks up to the ceiling before facing me. "I don't have plans, but I also won't be here to feed Oscar."

"Who's Oscar?"

She throws her hands up. "My fish, Vance! I thought you knew everything about me?"

I do. I mean, I did know about the fish, but its name wasn't in her record, and I don't recall her ever saying it in my presence.

I give her a little push to get moving and wave away her concern. "Leave me your key, and I'll have Serena stop by and feed it."

She pulls to a stop, and I nearly plow her over. "Oh, hell no, that twatinator is not going in my house and rooting through all my belongings."

I grin. "First, I think you're exaggerating the definition of a house. Second, what is a twatinator?" If I wasn't so frustrated with her, I think I would have laughed at her folded arms and serious expression. "Is that like a southern term I'm not familiar with?"

She cocks her hip, and the pink patterned dress she has on pulls snug against her thighs, drawing my attention lower. "No, it isn't a southern term. It's just a term I made up so I don't call her what she really is."

I step in closer and whisper, "And what would that be?" Wanting her to say something inappropriate makes my dick hard. I haven't wanted a woman this bad in a very long time.

Noticing the change in my demeanor, she glances up and down my body, swallowing harshly.

"Tell me," I coax. "Tell me what you really think of Serena."

I'm thinking I'll need to linger at my house a little longer, possibly take a shower so I can think on this plane ride in Ms. Belle's flowered-smelling presence.

"I..." She swallows again, looking around.

"Serena left early today." She, too, was getting on my nerves.

"Oh. She wasn't sick, was she?"

"You're stalling." I push in closer, watching as her concern turns into aggravation.

"And you're now the one being inappropriate."

I take the last of the space between us. "Sucks, doesn't it?"

With my body within an inch of hers, she has to look up to flash me a glare. "I think Serena is a grade A cunt."

My dick jumps at the foul words coming out of such a sweet mouth.

"Are you happy now? Can we go?"

Look who's uncomfortable now. "Lead the way."

The motel is still as shitty as it was when I left this morning from picking her up.

"I'll be just a minute. I need to ask my neighbor if he'll feed Oscar for me."

The neighbor.

He's just a kid, Vance. Just. A. Fucking. Kid.

"I'll go with you."

Her head drops to her shoulders as if she's exhausted already. "No, stay here. I'm just going next door."

And I'll just be going next door, too. This isn't the kind of motel that you just let sweet, naive women wander around. "Fine," I lie. "I'll wait on you."

Exhaling, she smiles. "Thank you."

See? Completely gullible and easy prey.

I wait, watching her pack up the fish, like it can't be without a human for longer than eight hours, and walk it next door. She doesn't even notice me coming after her.

Leaning against the wall outside the kid's door, I listen as she rambles on and on about what size a pinch of food is. Apparently, the fish is an overeater, and she has him on a diet. It's the most absurd thing I've heard this year.

"Thank you, dude. Seriously, I owe you. When I get back in town, we'll grab lunch, yeah?"

The hell she will.

Ms. Belle will have lunch meetings until she earns that stupid thousand dollars she has left. This "kid" might be young, be he's not too young to notice her soft curves and fine edges. You don't end up in a pay-by-the-hour motel for no reason.

Halle leans in and makes this sound, and I'm yanking her from a hug before I realize what I've done.

"Vance!" she scolds, smoothing her dress and flashing the baby a regretful look.

Ask me how much I give a shit. "We need to leave. We don't have time for all your damn hugs."

For a moment, I think I've hurt her feelings, but then she narrows her eyes at me and points her finger. "Go wait for me in my room."

I chuckle. No one tells me what to do, even sweet little things that make my dick rock solid. "Finish saying goodbye." I give her no indication I'm moving from this spot until then.

We lock glares for a moment, then she lets out this long sigh and turns back to the boy. "You have my number, right?"

He nods, never taking his harsh stare off me. One day, kid, you'll be old enough to be a threat but never to me. Ms. Belle may take pity on you, but you'll never get a chance to slide your fingers between her legs and hear her whimper for more. Not like I will.

"Okay, good. Call me if you have any questions or if you just want to chat. I'll probably be bored. I don't know what you even do at a conference held at a winery."

You talk. You drink. You fuck.

It's pretty simple and the only reason Astor attends. But I don't burst her bubble about her precious boss. She's already upset enough with this whole plane fiasco. Astor and his stupid visuals.

"I'm sure your boss won't mind keeping you company." The second pain in my ass shoots me a dark look, which sends Halle doubling over in a fit of laughter.

"Vance isn't my boss," she tries explaining through pants of laughter. "And he'd rather push me from the plane than spend more time with me than he has to."

A knot settles in my stomach at her admission. "And yet, I'm the one keeping you from being fired." And having an episode on the plane. I wouldn't exactly classify that as a dick move.

"I'm sorry, Vance. I didn't mean it that way. I was only joking. You're right, you've been so kind helping me with all of this."

The teenager in front of her snorts. "I'm sure kindness was exactly why he offered to escort you onto his private jet."

If I could form a relationship with anyone right now, I would have agreed with the kid's observation. A few years ago, that's exactly what I was doing. Wooing women on my personal jet while we contributed to burning through the ozone layer with our self-satisfying carbon footprint. But now, with trembling hands in my pocket from looking over the file in Duke's office earlier… Suffice it to say, my game with women has long since abandoned me.

"It's not like that—" she tries explaining before he cuts her off.

"Call me Rem." He shoots me a narrowed glare. "My name is Remington."

For some reason, this makes Halle smile. "Remington," she repeats like she's trying out his name for the first time.

"Did you not know his name?" I find myself asking.

She shakes her head, stepping up to Remington and taking back the hug I pulled her from earlier. "Thank you, Remington. I owe you."

This whole conversation makes me want to bash my head against the brick wall, but fortunately, Halle takes pity on me and steps back. "I'll be back on Saturday. Kay?"

Remington, whose name we all know now, nods, tipping his chin as she climbs into the passenger seat.

"See you later, kid. Don't drown the fish." Or yourself. It'd only keep Halle here longer.

He spares me no mind as he smiles back at Halle, pulling out a cigarette and addressing me quietly. "Make her cry, and I'll flush your career down with the fish."

This kid has balls.

I'm impressed.

Too bad his threat means nothing. You can't threaten a man who has nothing left to lose.

I lost my career a year ago.

At this point, I'm only here to save Duke and Astor's.

The plane is waiting on the tarmac by the time we arrive.

"Do you have a paper bag?"

Halle's been quiet the whole ride here. Normally, her silence is ideal, but since she probably suffers from PTSD, I worry she's retreating into herself. Though, asking for something is a good sign.

"No, I don't have a paper bag. Do you feel like you're going to hyperventilate or barf?" Unlocking the doors, I reach for our bags in the back, keeping my eyes on her just in case she's getting sick.

"Barf?" She arches a brow at me. "That's an unusual word for you, isn't it?"

I fight off the urge to grin. "I think you, of all people, Ms. Belle, should know I can use slang without issue."

Her cheeks tint with pink, and I know she's remembering the night she was pantyless, spread out beneath me as I lied and claimed I could remain professional at the sight of her pussy. It was one of the hardest things I've ever had to do. It wasn't just the sight of her pussy on my floor, but the smell of her arousal as she fought through the pain as I stretched her. It was sensory overload.

Being with her on this plane, forty thousand feet in the air... isn't much better.

"Are you sure you didn't bring any sedatives?" Her fear has returned.

Closing the door, I walk around to her side and squat down so I'm at eye level. "You don't need a sedative."

I don't tell her I have one just in case. You don't specialize in scar revisions and not encounter patients who have traumatic pasts. I didn't realize Halle would have a sensitivity to planes; her file didn't mention it, but regardless, I'm prepared to get her to Astor safely, both mentally and physically.

"I don't want you to see me like this or worse," she finally says, her gaze tracking to the ground.

My chest tightens as I put a finger under her chin and lift her eyes back to mine. "See you like what?"

Her lips quiver. "Broken."

"You're not broken." Leaning in, I smooth the lines of her mouth with my thumb. "Never broken, Peach."

A tear streaks down her face as her hand clings to mine. "You don't know me. I wasn't," she sniffles, "I wasn't always like this."

"Like what?"

Releasing me, she extends her hand between us. I don't think either one of us breathes when she places her hand over my heart and whispers, "Brave. I wasn't always brave… until I saw you."

I swear my heart spasms, sending my rhythm into atrial fibrillation.

"When I was lying there in that hospital bed and couldn't move— couldn't breathe without pain. All I could think was I wanted to die. My friends were his. My apartment… Starting over. Learning to walk seemed impossible."

She blinks and more tears fall. "And then one night, after a very painful therapy session, I saw you. You were giving an interview on TV with that woman whose husband set her on fire."

I nod, remembering the woman well. She was one of my first patients after I rebranded the practice. Lois was her name.

"She said you…" A sob shudders through her.

"We don't need to talk about this right now."

She swipes at the tears and shakes her head stubbornly. "She said you heard her screams in the hospital and came to her. You sat and held her hand as they cleaned her burns."

I can still hear her screams as they debrided her wounds.

Halle's hands rest on my face as she forces my gaze to hers. "She said you gave her the strength to keep living—to keep fighting for her future."

"That was a long time ago," I try explaining. "I'm not—"

"She was beautiful, showing off her scars that were still there but refined." Her bottom lip quivers as she shakes her head, cutting me off. "She called you *the* Potter. A man who took lumps of clay and shaped them into something beautiful."

"I don't want to hear the rest of this story." I try pulling away, my heart pounding in my chest. But Halle ignores my protests and grips my shirt, holding me still.

"And I knew just by looking at you up there, so humble, so awkward, that one day I would meet you, and you would become my potter, too."

Fuck it. I kiss her.

CHAPTER TWENTY

Vance

"Vance," Halle breathes against my lips. Her sapphire blue eyes are wide with shock as she pulls back, seeing her shirt fisted in my hand. I don't remember grabbing her or pulling her onto my lap. I just remember Halle not being close enough.

And that was a problem.

A *big* fucking problem.

Kissing Halle is a career-ending move. Yet, as I lap up the salty tears streaming down her face, I can't force myself to care.

"You don't need a potter." I breathe along her wet skin, the smell more intoxicating than bourbon. "You're already perfection."

Halle makes a soft noise, her lips parting on an exhale. "I'm not perf—"

"Don't," I scold before pressing my lips back to hers. No matter what Halle thinks about her body, she'll never see herself the way I do. "I don't want to hear any more," I admit.

I just want to indulge this *need* I have for Halle. This feeling of wholeness with her wrapped in my arms while her body relaxes under my hands as my fingers slip underneath her shirt, lingering at the clasp of her bra.

Unhooking it would be a mistake, and I'm already straddling the line of complications by kissing Ms. Belle. Taking this moment further would obliterate whatever minuscule amount of professionalism I have left.

But damn, she fits perfectly against me.

Her soft body molds to my rigid hardness, merging her curves with mine.

Maybe Halle was on to something with the whole *potter* thing. I *do* want to mold her, but only against my body, keeping her tucked to my chest—safe and untainted by the words of a fallen society. She might think her scars make her less than perfect, but I didn't become a plastic surgeon to fit women and men into society's mold. I specialized in reconstruction to give them the confidence they need to ignore the stigmas of how perfection and beauty are defined.

Perfection is unattainable.

Beauty is in words, actions, and life.

Halle might have found me to erase a part of her that she'd rather not remember, but I'll rest easy knowing she'll leave me with the knowledge that she's no less beautiful than she was before.

Her fight is exquisite.

Her resilience is magnificent.

And her body is… beautifully flawed and perfectly crafted. Exactly what my dreams are made of.

"We need to go," I finally mutter after several moments of lazily exploring Halle's mouth, nuzzling her neck as her hair falls over my cheek, enveloping me in a false sense of security. But no matter how well we fit together, Halle is not here for anything more than a scar revision. It'd serve me well to remember that before this weekend gets out of hand.

"Okay." Halle's words are hesitant and unsure as she untangles her hands from my hair.

Her sheer vulnerability has me leaning forward, finding her lips once more, pressing gently until she moans, stealing my breath. My stomach tightens with a weird sensation that has me breaking contact. "I need to grab our things," I slide her off my lap and help her to her feet. "Do you think you can board without me?"

Not that I won't be right behind her, but I need to know she isn't going to pass out when my hands are full of the fucking pamphlets Astor couldn't remember to take with him.

Halle blinks several times as if she's clearing something from her eyes. "I'll be fine."

"You sure?"

She nods and then turns around, grabbing her bag from the back seat. "I'll see you on board, Dr. Potter."

Dr. Fucking Potter.

Why does her saying my name like that make me want to grab her and toss her on the hood of the car and fuck her until she's not even aware that we're getting on a plane?

Because I've slipped.

Somehow, I've let this woman wear me down. Calista would love to seize this lapse in judgment and further taint my reputation during this lawsuit.

Keep your head on straight, Vance.

"If you're sure," I confirm, reaching for another bag inside the car. "I'll be right behind you."

Inhaling, Halle squares her shoulders in a look of pure determination before turning and walking toward the plane. I watch her for several breaths as she approaches the stairs and stops.

Keep going, Halle. Don't stop.

But she does, dropping her bag onto the ground and turning around, her lips parted in an apology. "I'm sorry, I don't think I can."

I let Astor's shit fall to the ground as I eat up the steps between Halle and me, scooping her up and enjoying the breathy gasp she lets out as her legs wrap around my waist. I carry Halle up the stairs, keeping focused on getting us inside without further incident. The flight attendant can grab our bags.

135

"Vance," Halle whispers, tucking her face into my neck, tightening her arms around me as we enter the cabin.

An ache spreads through my chest as I hold her close. I know what she's feeling all too well. When you have no control over your body as the silent demon within takes over without your consent.

"You're not alone," I assure Halle calmly, carefully moving down the aisle and coming to a stop at one of the leather chairs. "I'm going to put you down so I can pour us a drink, okay?"

I have a feeling we desperately need it.

She shakes her head. "I don't want to throw up." Her normally snarky tone has this brokenness that concerns me.

"Okay," I concede. "No alcohol. Guess we'll find another way to relax you."

She pulls back and offers me a half-hearted smile. "Told you I'd need the sedatives."

I adjust her up my body and turn, taking us both down to the leather chair. "You disappoint me, Ms. Belle. I thought you, of all people, would have realized I never lose an argument."

Except to Calista. But that's a different game altogether.

Halle's smile tilts upward, looking more like the real Halle I've come to know over the past few weeks. "I think you overestimate your ability, Dr. Potter. I think it's more like you haven't been challenged properly."

She's playing a dangerous game.

One that will leave her spent beneath me.

Lifting her chin with one finger, I situate her on my lap, grinding her down on my hard cock. "I should warn you, Ms. Belle, challenging me never leaves my opponents happy."

Halle leans forward, her earlier hesitation dissipating as she threads her fingers through my hair and tilts my face upward. "Are you flirting with me, Dr. Potter?"

The flight attendant stows our bags—and the fucking pamphlets—and closes the cabin door before I can respond. Halle flinches, turning back, her chest rising and falling in short pants. "Oh, God. I don't think I can do this."

"You *will* do this," I tell her, holding her hips to mine as she tries to stand.

Her eyes are wide with panic. "Vance, please. Tell Astor I'm sorry."

I'm telling Astor no such thing. This woman, who took a bus cross-country to deal with a man in a perpetual bad mood, is no quitter. "When we get there, you can tell Astor to bring his own shit next time." I pull the seat belt around her, securing us both to the seat in a quick motion.

"Oh, God." She buries her face into my neck as the engine whirls to life.

Her body is tense, shivering in my arms. If she keeps this up, I will have to sedate her. There's a fine line between dealing with PTSD and making it worse. If I don't distract Halle quickly, I'll have no other choice. I can't allow her to suffer.

Pulling her higher up my thighs, I rub my palms up and down her back, placing a kiss to her hair and whispering, "I black out sometimes."

My random, awkward declaration does the trick as Halle lifts her head slowly.

Fuck, what are you doing, Vance? Calming her or attending confession?

"What do you mean you *black out?*"

The plane begins to taxi the runway, but Halle doesn't seem to notice. She's now completely latched on to the dark skeleton I work hard to keep out of the limelight.

"Is that what happened the day I found you in the bathroom?"

So curious…

"Yes." This method of indulging my secrets to distract her is clearly working, but not for me. Now, I'm the one with the racing heart and tight chest.

"Just, yes? Seriously, Vance."

I'd be relieved her attitude is back if it wasn't at the expense of me elaborating. "You asked me a question, and I answered it. What more do you want to know?"

Halle's lip twitches as she fights off a smile. "Well, since you asked…"

Wrong thing to say, dumbass.

"I'd like to know when these blackouts started."

I growl out my displeasure at this line of questioning, but it doesn't seem to bother Halle. I swallow and look out the window, seeing we are now in the air. At least she doesn't seem to notice.

"Vance," she turns my head toward her. "How long?"

"A while."

She quirks a brow, her hands going to my shoulders, kneading the tension there. "A while as in a year ago?"

I snap my gaze to hers. "What do you know about last year?"

Someone's been fucking talking, and I intend to put an end to it as soon as we land. There's no way Halle could know about Logan. Could she? Not without my brothers telling her, and they wouldn't. They know how sacred the Potter secrets are. If one falls, we all fall.

"I don't know anything about what happened last year. Just that you changed from the man I heard about to the man you are now."

Ah. Well, she could have easily figured that out. The critical piece of information, she's still missing. And I plan to keep it that way.

"Did what happen to you last year cause the blackouts?"

It's an innocent question. One a friend would ask. Are Halle and I friends? I'm not so sure. We've helped each other during difficult situations, but these situations wouldn't be as difficult if she'd just taken no for an answer the first time we met.

We wouldn't be here on a plane with me calming her PTSD symptoms with stories of my own.

I sigh and lean my head back against the seat, my gaze drifting to the ceiling. "Yes. My therapist calls them psychogenic blackouts."

My throat bobs as the weight lifts from my chest just by speaking the words aloud. The psychogenic attacks aren't something my brothers and I talk about. That's what I pay a therapist for. However, telling someone else, who can understand, holds a certain freedom I didn't know existed.

"Oh, Vance..."

All I can feel is her heat on my thighs as she leans in, pressing her lips against mine. I want out of this feeling. I don't need another friend.

Sharing horror stories leads to bonds. And I can't afford to destroy another soul.

But her moans…

I find it impossible to ignore anything regarding Ms. Belle.

"Can I touch you?" Her words are a whispered plea to both of our ears.

"No." I nip at her neck. "You're gonna let me touch you, Ms. Belle."

Her back arches, moaning out. "Yes. Be inappropriate with me, Dr. Potter. Please."

No one has ever spoken more convincing words.

Unlatching the seatbelt, I wrap an arm around Halle's back, holding her still while I snake my free hand down the front of her pants, stretching the waistband until I reach the wetness I seek.

Her flesh is scorching as I slide two fingers between her folds, dragging the wetness around to her sensitive nub.

"Oh, shit." She bucks in my arms, and rather than risk her falling, I take us to the floor, the vibrations from the turbulence sending jolts of pleasure through us both. "Is this inappropriate enough for you, Ms. Belle?"

Curling my finger, I press the rippled flesh inside her as her legs wrap around my back. "No." She pants. "I think you can do so much worse."

I look down and find her eyes closed with a ridiculous grin on her face. "This is why I would have never hired you," I scold.

Scissoring my fingers, I stretch out my employee for a second time. This time, it's not her hips. Though, at this point, I wouldn't be opposed to stretching those either. I want to ruin and rebuild everything there is about Halle Belle, her sass included.

Halle's hands graze my chest as she cups me between the legs. "Why wouldn't you hire me, Dr. Potter? Is it because you would be the one who couldn't remain professional?"

She squeezes my cock in her hand, and I bow over, letting my head hit the floor. "I think we've both established we have poor professionalism."

And work ethics if we're being honest.

Halle Belle was sent here to break me, and she just might succeed.

But right here, right now, with my fingers so deep inside this sassy southern belle, finger-fucking her without abandon while her body coats my fingers in juices, I know I won't go down without casualties. Namely, her.

CHAPTER TWENTY-ONE

Halle

"You're kinda giving me stalker vibes."

I grin over my shoulder at Vance, who hovers behind me, watching as I attempt to smooth my hair into something more presentable in the plane's small bathroom mirror.

It looks like I've been riding atop the plane and not my doctor's fingers like I was in a Texan rodeo with eight seconds to prove myself.

I'm sweaty, my hair is tangled, and my clothes are damp.

I'm a freaking sexed-up mess.

And I'm pretty sure I like it.

"Stalker." He hides his grin behind his hand. "I'm pretty sure you're confusing our roles. I'm not the one who refused to return home after receiving no for an answer."

I knew he would bring that up. Problem is, I have absolutely no shame in what I did by staying in Texas after he refused to be my surgeon. I needed surgery, and Vance was the man I picked. His refusal was never in the plan. I would have thought he would have become accustomed to the idea by now.

I flash him a smile in the mirror. "The word *no* I find to be subjective."

Vance takes a step forward and presses his front to my back. "Subjective, huh?" He pulls the hair from my fingers, gathering it in one hand, and moving it to the opposite shoulder.

I swallow as he gazes at his fingers trailing along the line of my neck, the movement predatory-like. "Yes, the dictionary is merely a suggestion." My voice cracks, and the words come out as an eccentric ramble while Dr. Potter's head lowers, and his lips press against my skin.

"Are you okay?"

Fortunately, I'm not too far gone to understand what he says, considering he asks the question while never pulling his lips from my skin. The pressure from his lips goes straight to my center.

I reach over my head and secure my hands behind his head, holding him to my neck, where I shamelessly watch him kiss me. "I'm fine, thanks to you."

I'm more than fine, really. Vance effectively kept me distracted the entire ride from Bloomfield to Napa. He was so sweet and generous with his words and… body. Honestly, I think all medical schools should teach doctors the skills of distraction like Vance possesses. It's quite refreshing—much better than a sedative.

"Your boss is probably waiting," he murmurs, looking like the last thing he wants to do is leave the plane and ride the short distance to the winery, where the conference is being held.

"You know, I can take it from here. You don't have to personally deliver me to Astor."

Always hiding his true feelings, Vance straightens. "Who said I was delivering you? The car is here for you, not me."

He's full of adorable shit. "Then, why did you bring a bag?"

Smirking, he turns around and walks out of the lavatory without a word.

It isn't until we pull up to the winery that excitement hits me square in the chest. "This place is gorgeous."

"Mhmm."

Vance has gone back to being his tense and broody self all in the span of ten minutes. It's certainly disheartening, considering his earlier mood on the plane. Where'd that Vance go? The one who joked and smiled. The one who played my body like an expensive instrument?

"Do you not like wineries?" I ask as our driver turns into the entrance.

"I don't like medical conferences." His voice seems far away as he stares out the window—a beautifully broken mirage of pain.

"Do you want to talk about it?"

Turning to face me, Vance offers me a smile. "I suggest you try the wine tasting at six o'clock. It's one of the best around."

He doesn't offer to go with me, and I'm too chicken to ask. I need to remember that while Vance sank his fingers deep inside me and made me feel alive for the first time in years, he's my doctor, first and foremost. And faced with his patient possibly having a PTSD episode, he did what he had to do to keep me calm.

"I'll do that," I tell him. "If it's anything like the entrance of this place, it'll be magnificent."

Vance doesn't bother answering or even smiling, for that matter. He simply gets out of the car, opens the trunk, and grabs the box of pamphlets while the driver helps me out. "I'll check us in while you find Astor."

Vance looks at the bellhop approaching. "Ms. Belle is looking for Dr. Astor Potter." He places the box in his arms and turns to me, his face rigid like the first time we met. "I'll find you later."

His statement comes out like an order, and I don't bother arguing to go with him. Clearly, something is troubling him, and he needs space to work it out. Normally, I would use the power of persuasion to convince him, but not today. After what Vance and I shared on the plane, I owe him the space to face his own demons. I will be here for him just like he was for me.

"Okay. I'll see you inside then." I would hug him since he really looks like he could use one, but he walks off before I can.

"Ms. Belle." The bellhop—is he a bellhop or a valet? I can't tell. Uppity is not a language I speak or even care to study. So, I'll just refer to this nice man carrying the box of pamphlets as a really sweet guy. "If you'll follow me, I'll take you to Dr. Potter."

His saying Dr. Potter makes me think of Vance, since he's the only one referred to by that name. At work, we refer to Astor as Dr. Astor and Duke as Dr. Duke. I wonder if, at these types of events, they all are referred to as Dr. Potter. Seems like things could get confusing.

I follow behind the nice man into the grand banquet hall full of more crystals than Kim Kardashian's closet, weaving through the expensive suits and pencil skirts. Gah, it feels stuffy in here. Like bad conversations and terrible perfume. No wonder Vance doesn't like these conferences. Who would in these conditions?

I finally find an opening, where I spot Astor easily. He seems out of place with his shirt unbuttoned at the top and his tie hanging loosely. He's like the bad boy on the yearbook committee. "I can take it from here," I tell my helper, taking the box from his hands and offering my sincerest thank you. I really could have carried the box myself, but since Vance was already in a mood, I didn't think it would be wise to insist. But now, with Vance not here to witness me taking the last few steps to Astor while carrying the box, I go all in. Just call me a rebel.

"Astor," I call out, making my way toward the best boss ever.

"You made it." Vance's charming brother reaches me quickly, taking the box from my hands. "You didn't carry this all the way from the car, did you?"

I take it back. He's not more charming than Vance. They both are Neanderthals.

"No, the man up front carried it."

Astor's eyes narrow as if he's weighing whether I'm lying or not.

"If you don't believe me, ask Vance. He's the one who made him carry it."

Astor sucks in a breath. "Vance came with you. Here?"

I nod slowly. "Was he not supposed to?"

"No, it's just…" Astor scans the room, dropping the box on the floor. "I need to warn him."

Okay, what in the serious heck is going on here? "Warn him about what?"

Astor shakes his head, not elaborating, and starts walking. And being the great employee I am, I follow. "He said he was checking us in."

Astor's eyes widen. "You're both staying?"

What's going on here? I hurry to catch up with Astor's long strides. "What's wrong? Is this place haunted?"

Astor pulls to a stop, and I run into him like a linebacker. "Oh, fuck."

I peer around Astor, just long enough to see Vance at the front desk, his body tense and rigid as if he's seen a ghost.

"Who is she?" I whisper to Astor, pointing at the woman who stands in front of him, tears streaming down her face as she trembles. "Astor." I shake the good doctor in my way. "Who is she?"

And why is she looking at Vance like she'd love nothing more than to spit in his face?

"She's…"

In the same breath, the woman rears back and slaps Vance across the face before walking off. "No, she fucking didn't."

I try charging past Astor to get to the bitch who can't seem to keep her hands to herself when Vance turns and spots us, one side of his face already reddening from her hand. "Your room key," is all he says as he tips his chin to Astor and taps the desk where a card sits.

"Vance, wait," I call out as he walks off, but Astor grabs my hand.

"I think we should give him some time," he suggests.

I nod, watching as he disappears down the hall. "Does that mean we can go after the cunt who hit him then?"

Astor turns around, grabbing me by the shoulders. "Do all Georgia girls have a mouth like yours?"

145

I force a smile. Who is this woman, and what makes her think she can hit Vance? I mean, most days, he probably deserves it, but not today. Not when he was being kind and… real. "No." I sigh. "Just the really special ones."

It's been three hours, and I can't find Vance anywhere.

"He won't answer his cell."

Unlocking my phone, I stare at it for the billionth time as if Vance will suddenly break pattern and call me back this time.

"I'm sure he's found a nice bottle of bourbon to occupy himself." Astor pats me on the shoulder, but with a quick look, I notice his gaze is scanning the conference room, too.

"I've never seen him look so…"

"Destroyed," Astor adds without elaborating.

"Who is that woman to Vance?" Obviously, they knew each other.

Astor sighs, giving me one last pat before stepping away, his eyes full of apologies. "I'll go look for Vance. Why don't you enjoy the wine tasting?"

It's the same thing Vance suggested earlier and the last thing I want to do right now. Something happened between Vance and that woman, and even though I'd like to know what all transpired, I'll take just knowing he's okay.

Vance Potter might be a jerk on most days, but deep down, he cares about people. And this woman ruined all the progress I've made with the moody surgeon.

"Call me if you find him, okay?" I don't bother agreeing to the wine tasting. I'll be searching for his brother on my own. It's my fault he's at this conference in the first place. If I didn't freak out over the flight, then he wouldn't have needed to come with me.

But he did.

Because he cares.

And I refuse to let him suffer alone. If Vance can drop what he's doing to help me, then I can do the same for him. Because that's what employees and employers do. Okay, so that's not necessarily true, but it sounds like an excuse Vance would use, and that's enough justification for me.

"Sure," Astor agrees, lifting a finger as he walks away, heading toward the bar.

When's he's out of sight, I take a deep breath and exhale slowly.

If I were a rude, antisocial surgeon, where would I go?

The bar? Astor is checking there.

The plane? No. It's likely sitting on an airstrip or wherever planes park and wait for people to fly them.

He could have taken a car...

If that's the case, the possibilities are endless, and I'd be more likely to find my missing sock from last week than I would Vance. But I need to do something. If I sit here, I'll just worry and feel guilty about not being able to get on a private jet alone—a dream most anyone would love to experience.

But I'm not most people.

I have demons, and clearly, Dr. Potter does, too.

And everyone knows when you live with demons, you need a demon slayer in your back pocket. Mine is Oscar and on planes, Vance. And Vance's demon slayer is... likely bourbon. But that's unhealthy, so today, his demon slayer will be me, whether he likes it or not.

Forming somewhat of a plan, I head to the back of the resort, where the rooms are. I don't expect Vance to be here because he never makes anything simple, but I'm going to check anyway. You never know, people can surprise you.

But after doing a thorough sweep of the floor and lying to the cleaning lady that my boss needed his phone from his room, I came up empty. Vance wasn't in his room or the hallways. Not that I really expected him to be in any of those places, but still, I was disappointed. Even as I walked back to the bars and winery.

Maybe Astor found him and they're enjoying a heart-to-heart? Who am I kidding? Vance doesn't do heart-to-hearts. He does snarky and rude. It's more likely Astor is grinning as Vance berates him for coming to his aid as if he were some toddler who wandered too far away.

But when I check a couple of the popular bars within the resort, I find them empty of any Potter brothers. I try calling Astor with no luck. It looks like now, both surgeons have put me on do not disturb.

Which irks me for all of a few seconds.

Astor is my boss. He doesn't report to me, therefore, he isn't required to answer his cell, even though I think it's tacky he doesn't. Vance, well, I expect such things from him. Vance doesn't do anything he doesn't want to. Especially when it comes to me.

But all those reasons don't keep me from calling their phones another dozen times before Astor finally picks up. "Yeah?" he answers, his voice breathy.

"Astor?" Pausing for a moment, I listen for anything that sounds suspicious. "Are you okay?"

"Mhmm…"

Some things you just know, and I know without a doubt that I've disturbed Astor mid-pork session.

Rage flows through me when I hear something like a groan. "I'm taking it you didn't find Vance?"

A grunting sound is followed up by a mumbled shush, which could only be Astor trying to quiet his after-conference meal.

"Never mind," I snap. "Enjoy. I'll find your brother myself."

His chuckle is the only thing that keeps me from screaming when he says, "Attagirl, Hal. Teamwork makes the dream work."

Yeah, I hang up on the bastard. He might be used to his brother disappearing, looking like someone ripped out his soul, but I'm not. Vance wouldn't be here without me, which, I realize, Astor wouldn't know. As he shouldn't since it only shows that I'm not a very good secretary.

Storming out of the bar, I head outside. I doubt he'll be in the vineyards or even lounging in one of the cozy rockers on the terrace, but it's worth a shot.

So far, Vance is a damn ghost. A very rude and angry ghost.

A ghost that I never find.

Not in the vineyard and not on the terrace.

It's dark by the time I finally give up. Wherever Vance is, it's a good hiding place. He was probably amazing at hide-and-seek when he was a kid.

I'm hungry, tired, and a little disappointed in my hunting skills by the time I unlock my room and find Dr. Potter on the floor....

Beautiful and broken.

CHAPTER TWENTY-TWO

Vance

The floor is fuzzy.

I hope that means I'm drunk enough to endure the upcoming lecture spewing out of Halle's lips.

Her lips...

They are everything a plastic surgeon could ever hope of achieving. Full and plump, even on the top and bottom. They. Are. Perfection.

"Are you going to answer me?" She folds her arms, arching her brows expectantly.

"I think you've known me long enough to know the answer to that question," I tell her, which only seems to upset her more as she pushes off the door and comes to straddle me on the floor.

"You know, Dr. Potter, I've had just about enough of your alpha bullshit."

Scoffing, I struggle to hold her glare. "Get out of my room."

A grin spreads along her face slowly. It makes me nervous. "You're in *my* room, Vance."

What? No.

I look around, noting the same white comforter and glass sitting on the table. But then I spot it, a pink bag slung over the chair.

Fuck.

I groan and try pushing up, only to be pushed back down. "How'd you get in my room, Vance?" She fingers my tie, a gentle smile on her face until I don't answer.

Suddenly, she pulls me forward.

"What are you doing?" I eye my tie clutched in her hand, noting the weight of her body over my legs, holding me captive.

"You answer my question and then I'll answer yours."

My hands go to her hips. "Don't make this embarrassing, Ms. Belle."

She throws her head back, and I swear her laughter feels like it comes from all around me. "Embarrassing for who? You, who can barely sit up, or me, who caught her boss shitfaced in her hotel room?"

"I thought this was my room."

Her gaze lowers. "How did your key work?"

Just when I thought this day couldn't get shittier. "I…" I exhale a deep breath, glimpsing her grip still tight on my tie. "I mixed up the room numbers."

"Still doesn't explain the key working."

Why? Why, Vance? Could you not have just rented a car and gone home? Why did you have to drown your sorrows in a bottle?

Clenching my teeth, I face her. "I might have passed out by your door, and the maintenance guy found me and ushered me in when I told him my keycard wouldn't work."

She laughs, loosening her grip enough where I can lean back against the wall. "The security here is pretty shitty."

I shrug. "I rented the whole wing. Technically, all these rooms are mine for the evening. I simply forgot which one I let you have."

"You did what?" She rocks back on her heels, her palms going to her thighs, drawing my gaze to her center, where my fingers were earlier. "You're telling me you rented all the rooms on this hall because you didn't want to run into anyone… else?"

I nod tightly, and it makes me dizzy. "I suppose the next thing you're going to ask me is why?"

Her breath hitches as she stares at me. "No, I know why."

"You have no idea." I try lifting her by her hips to stand, but her hands atop of mine stop me.

"You're right. I have no idea why you would go through so much trouble renting all the rooms when you could have just taken the jet back home and left me with Astor."

My jaw tightens on the last bit of her sentence. "You've never been to Napa. You should see it since you had to come anyway."

Her delicate brow arches. "And this is your way of showing me Napa?"

Haha. "No, I didn't intend to see Napa *with* you. I'm merely your hands-off travel agent."

This time, she laughs a full belly laugh. "My hands-off travel agent, huh?"

I nod, not seeing why she thinks this is so hilarious. Well, I can, but I'm not in the mood to endure her teasing. "Get up."

She sobers instantly. "No."

"No?"

"You heard me." Her eyes challenge me, and I am ready for it.

"Ms. Belle," I clear my throat, "if you don't get up, you're fired."

"I don't work for you."

She thinks that statement and sexy grin will stop me. Astor doesn't care enough about this practice to keep me from firing his secretary. I can easily find him a replacement from a temp agency. She'd likely be able to fly alone, too. "Ms. Belle, I'm going to count to four—"

"Thank you," she blurts out, cutting off the rest of my threat.

"What?"

Her throat works as she wrings her hands in front of her. "I said, thank you. I know you'd rather be at home, away from all these surgeons and whoever that awful woman is, but I'm thankful you're here. I'm not sure if you're still here because you're forcing yourself to stay in order to distract me on the plane ride back or if you are too tired to leave tonight."

I open my mouth to speak, but she stops me with a finger to my lips. "Either way, I really appreciate it. No one has ever done something so sweet. Not for me."

Suddenly, the alcohol-induced fog clears, and I want to strangle the asshole in her file. Instead, I act like the asshole I am. "You don't want my kindness, Peach."

"That sounds like a threat, Dr. Potter."

I lift one shoulder. "Nothing good comes from me being sweet. It's best if you remember that." All I can offer her is the truth. When I've been kind, people have suffered.

Without so much as another word, Halle simply tips her chin in agreement or defiance—who knows with her—and stands, offering me her hand. "Come on, Dr. Potter. Let's get you sober so you can show me around Napa."

I narrow my gaze. "Didn't I say I was hands-off?"

She grabs my hand and pulls in a weak attempt to help me stand. "Well, I'm not going to let you sit here and destroy your liver next to my bed."

Reluctantly, I take her hand, seeing how her standing over me only creates a distraction with her dress. "Fine. I'll destroy my liver in my own room." Straightening my shirt and tie, I try standing taller. "My apologies for the confusion."

She rolls her eyes and pulls me by my belt. "Come on, I'm hungry, and I don't know a good place to eat."

"Room service," I say dryly.

"Cute, but I'm thinking I'm hungry for something a little more… salty. I think it'll work wonders on that attitude of yours."

She shoves me hard, and my knees hit the back of the bed before I fall. "What the—"

Halle is on me in a second, kissing my mouth, my jaw, until she gets to my neck. "You were a tease on the plane, Dr. Potter."

"I was distracting you," I argue futilely as she kisses the corner of my mouth, teasing me by not giving me the contact I didn't know I needed.

"And now, I'm distracting *you*. Tit for tat and all that."

My head is spinning while she unbuttons my shirt, lifting my undershirt over my head and leaving it over my eyes. "I can't see," I grumble, wrestling one arm out before she stops me by grabbing my hand and placing it on her bare breast. At least, that's what I think it is, considering I can't confirm it.

"You don't need to see, Vance. Just *feel.*"

I can fucking do that. *I can* so *do that.* Palming her tit in my hand, I roll her hardened nipple between my fingers. "You're the boss, Peach."

And for the first time in a very long time, I don't mind not being the one in charge as Halle unbuttons my pants and slides them and my boxers down to my ankles.

"Stroke yourself," she whispers at my ear, easing down my body and kneeling between my thighs "Show me how the famous doctor loses control."

She drags a hand down my chest, stopping to kiss my waist, her tongue sweeping over the sensitive skin until my hips buck.

I'm regretting giving her this control. "I can't—"

Warmth envelops my cock. Wet, controlled pulls send my head back to the mattress, my neck straining with every torturous lick.

"Give me your hand, Dr. Potter."

At this point, she could ask me for anything, and I would do it. My dick hasn't felt a mouth in a year. Clearly, we've missed it since I place my hand in hers. She closes my hand around my cock and then puts me between her lips, sliding all the way down until her lips meet my hand.

"Oh, fuck," I groan as she bobs up and down, her hands wrapping around mine as we milk my cock together. I'm in sensory overload, my hands trembling as I fight the urge to come down her throat mere minutes after starting.

"Vance," she says from around my dick, before easing off, the cool air hitting me like an arctic wind.

I almost whine and shout *what the fuck*, but then Halle takes my free hand and guides it to her head. "I want you to fuck my mouth, Dr. Potter."

My cock jumps in my hand, and I need to remember to breathe.

"I want to see you break."

I think we both can agree that she's seen me break more times than any other employee, but right now, with the heat of her mouth hovering over my cock, I'm not in the mood to deny her of anything.

Instead, I grip her hair in my hand and shove her down onto my cock, feeding her every inch of me until she gags.

My dick throbs as I work Halle's head up and down, meeting my hand thrust for thrust. Every muscle in my body is strung tight while my breathing turns into shallow pants. "Uncover my eyes," I plead. "I want to see you."

Halle wanted to see me break. Here it is. The need to see her swollen lips wrapped around my cock is truly unbearable. "Peach." My voice is a harsh growl as I lift Halle's mouth from my cock. "Let me see you."

I hear her chuckle before I feel her hands go to my knees and push up, her mouth at my ear in the next breath. "Don't stop stroking yourself, Dr. Potter, or I'll keep you blindfolded."

I grit my teeth, for once, keeping my attitude in check. The ultimate goal here is to see her. I'll do whatever it takes to accomplish this.

Nodding, I adjust my grip and slide my hand up my cock. Without the warmth and tug of her mouth, it doesn't feel the same.

"My patience is wearing thin," I tell her when the shirt still covers my eyes.

Her light chuckle only serves to infuriate me. "You're not the one in control here, Dr. Potter. I'm the boss, remember?"

Her hand wraps around mine, increasing the pressure around my dick as I slide up and down the shaft.

"Say it, Vance. Say I'm the boss."

Fuck me. I'm going to come in my hand like a teenager. "You're the boss," I grit, fighting off the tightening sensation in my balls. "Now, uncover my fucking eyes, and let me watch as I come down your pretty throat."

The shirt is ripped from my eyes. I blink away the blur, finding her swollen lips and a smirk that I crave to kiss. Hard. "You all right, Dr. Potter?"

She glances down my body, her gaze stopping at my fisted hand. "No, I need your help."

She kisses me, and immediately, my hand goes back into her hair, keeping her there.

Gripping her lips, she opens up farther, and I take the opening and devour her just like she's been doing to me.

"That's enough," she says, pulling away with a grin. She drags her tits down my chest, and I groan, the friction almost too much to handle. I'm nuclear, ready to explode at any minute.

"You wanted to come down my throat, didn't you?" She ties her hair back and settles herself back between my legs.

I swallow, trying to find the restraint not to toss her onto this bed and tie her up and pound into her sweet flesh until she comes on my cock.

But that's not what bosses do with their employees.

I ease up onto my elbow and slide my hands back into Halle's hair. "I do, but I'm not the boss here." I pull her head forward as I kiss and release her. "Do you want me to come in your mouth, Peach?"

My words have been utterly filthy, but I think we can all agree that Ms. Belle pulled them out of me, or it was the alcohol. It's hard to tell. Both make me crazy.

Halle leans her head into my palm, the soft skin of her cheek like satin on my hand. "I want to swallow all of you, Dr. Potter." She kisses the tips of my fingers. "Every. Last. Drop."

And so, she shall.

Guiding her head down, I take myself back into my hand, giving my cock a few strokes as she guides me into her mouth and pulls.

"Fuck." My head goes back against my will as Halle works me into a frenzy. My strokes are erratic as my back hits the mattress.

"Peach..."

She doesn't stop at my warning. Instead, her pulls become harder, and her hand wraps around mine.

The friction.

The intimacy of us together, bringing me to a point of madness, all becomes too much as I truly break, letting go deep inside Halle's throat.

As I lie there, stroking her hair as she eases off, gently kissing the head of my dick, I realize that Halle was never fragile. Never weak.

I should have known she would prove me wrong and show me she could handle anything I threw at her.

I just never thought it would be handling me.

Halle Belle, the southern girl from Georgia, just owned me.

And I'm not sure I care anymore.

CHAPTER TWENTY-THREE

Vance

"I'm freaking starving."

I arch a brow. "Didn't we just have this discussion? I seem to remember already satisfying your craving for something salty."

Her cheeks redden at my words. "Touché. But now, I'm hungry for *actual* food."

I eye the robe she's wearing, the knot loose around her waist. "I'll order room service—I wasn't joking when I said they had the best food—but only if you put on some clothes."

After I came so hard I nearly blacked out, Halle left me there on the bed to shower. It was a considerate move on her part. I had violated so many company rules that if I didn't own the practice, I would have fired me on the spot.

I'm ashamed of myself. Halle is not only my employee but my patient. Nothing good can ever come from sleeping with a patient.

Yet, here I am, my chest lighter, and my stomach ravenous for more than just food. Since Halle came into my office, it hasn't been so dark—so alone. I might be breaking the rules, but nothing feels wrong about spending time with Ms. Belle.

Halle grins, her long lashes batting with several blinks. "Are you saying you're embarrassed to be seen with me?"

I yank her by the knot of her robe, it easily falling open and baring her naked body underneath. The scars at her hips and thighs are pink under this ambient lighting. She's never looked more beautiful than she does in this moment.

"Embarrassed?" I trail a finger down her chest, her quick inhale spurring me lower. "No. Greedy? Yes."

I pinch her pert, pink nipple and enjoy the moan that goes through her. "No more inappropriate behavior on company time, Ms. Belle. I'd hate to have the bellhop fired on account of seeing your glorious body."

She swallows, her smile fading into a look I'm now all too familiar with. "Clothes. Now." I turn her around and smack her on the ass, pushing her toward the bathroom. "I'll order something."

Turning back, she asks, "What if I don't like what you order?"

For fuck's sake. Why can't this woman ever do as she's told?

"You'll like what I order." Because I'll order the entire menu if I must. She's eating something, even if I need to hand-feed her. "Now, please take mercy on me and cover up."

Her being clothed isn't only for the bellhop's sake. Unfortunately, my restraint is lacking with Ms. Belle on a good day. On a naked day, it's at negative zero.

Thankfully, Halle turns around and walks toward the bathroom but not before one last parting jab. "You know, I'm sort of liking this new, open, less growly Dr. Potter." She shrugs. "He's pretty cute."

Cute?

"Nothing about me is—"

She slams the door in my face, cutting off the rest of my argument and the all-access view of her incredible body.

"Oh, wow."

Halle leans back against the headboard and moans. "This is better than sex."

I cut her a look of disappointment. "I doubt that."

"You don't know that, Dr. Potter. I've had bad dick. It's not yummy. Not like this."

The mere mention of any dick other than mine in her life sends a weird tingling through my stomach. "It's just a chicken sandwich. I'm not seeing how that can be better than sex."

She takes another bite and holds out the sandwich. "Take a bite."

"No." I pull back so she can't shove the sandwich in my mouth.

"Don't tell me you're a germaphobe?" Her gaze narrows to my lips.

"I'm a doctor. I'm not scared of anything, especially not germs."

The arguments she has with me are about the most mundane topics I've ever endured, but it's better than being downstairs with my peers, who have probably heard about my run-in with Calista.

"I think you're lying." She moves closer, sitting up on her knees. "I think you'd rather my tongue be in your mouth or your fingers in my pussy, but you'd never stoop so low as to eat after—"

I bite the fucking sandwich and chew, swallowing it down quickly. "I still disagree. It isn't better than sex." I watch as her face morphs from shock to curiosity. "I don't like chicken. Especially not more than sex."

I don't have time for any more of her ridiculous conversations.

"Who doesn't like chicken?" She pulls the sandwich back and takes a bite, waiting for an answer to the most irrelevant question in the universe.

"I don't."

"Why?"

I shrug. "The texture bothers me."

She snaps back. "Isn't the texture the same as most meats?"

"No." I frown, getting back to my own meal—steak, not chicken.

"And you think *I'm* ridiculous." Halle laughs, taking a sip directly from the wine bottle I had sent up. She refuses to allow me to drink it as she claims I had my share of alcohol earlier, and my liver needs a rest.

I pretend to concede, only because she's probably right. Clearly, drunk Vance fucks up more than sober Vance when Halle is involved. It's probably best if I dry out before I do something really crazy like enjoy Ms. Belle's company more than I already do.

"So, tell me, Dr. Potter. What happened with you and Twat-tankerous earlier?"

A piece of food gets hung in my throat, and it takes me a few moments to clear it before I can reply. "I'm scared to ask what Twat-tankerous even means."

Halle waves me off, totally serious. "She's Serena's sister, isn't she? I knew the cunt didn't fall far from the cunt tree."

Setting my food down, I fight off a grin and take a deep breath. This isn't a conversation I want to have with an employee or a patient, but Halle's colorful use of derogatory nicknames has me answering just to see if she can come up with more. "No, Calista is not related to Serena."

"Calista sounds like she's bitchy, too."

I sigh and shove the food away before scooting up the bed and resting against the headboard. "She wasn't always. Years ago, we were inseparable."

Done with her food, too, Halle grabs the bottle of wine and moves in closer, handing me the bottle. I lift a brow. "Thought you said my liver needed a break?"

She shrugs, and I chug it before she can change her mind. If I plan on telling more of this story, then I definitely don't want to be sober. Can't have any of those pesky blackouts taking me down again in front of Halle. It's liable to ruin my less than stellar impression with my new patient.

When I can feel the alcohol working its way down my chest, I finally hand back the bottle. Halle takes it and she, too, chugs, gulping several times before she sets the bottle on the nightstand and looks over at me, her body coiling with tension. "Was she your girlfriend?" she asks carefully.

I bark out a laugh, feeling it deep inside my belly. "Calista? No." I shake my head. "She was always Logan's girl."

"Who's Logan?"

My chest seizes at the mention of his name, and I fight to breathe. "He was my best friend."

"Was?" Her voice is soft and full of pity. I don't like it.

"I killed him."

Always, the charmer, Vance. That's one way to get rid of Ms. Belle. This story will surely have her scrambling for another job and surgeon.

"I don't understand. How—" I just want this story, this confession, over. The sooner Halle knows the truth, the sooner she can move on with her life back in Georgia.

"Logan and I were childhood friends. Both of our fathers were surgeons, and we were expected to follow in their footsteps, just like Astor and Duke. We were all friends, going to the same country club every weekend."

I rake my hands through my hair, a fine sheen of sweat dotting my skin. "Calista's father owned the country club. I remember when she and Logan met." I chuckle. "At seventeen, Logan was an awkward bastard. He would watch Calista lying out on the pool chairs every afternoon in her yellow bikini. Then one day, he decided he was going to talk to her and took her a lemonade—her favorite." I burst out with genuine laughter at the memory. "He tripped, spilled the lemonade, and ended up splitting his lip on the edge of her chair. He bled all over that yellow bikini of hers."

I chuckle, but it doesn't feel authentic anymore.

"They fell in love after that?"

I chance a look at Halle and nod. "They were married during our second year of med school."

They were the couple who would have made it fifty years had it not been for me.

I swallow, knowing the next question she'll ask. "Two years ago, Logan was in a motorcycle accident." My voice cracks, and I have to cough to right it. "A year later, after his injuries healed, he asked me to refine a few of the scars. He was scared Calista would leave him because he didn't look the same anymore."

162

Halle's eyes gloss over as tears collect at the corners. I wipe them off, knowing she probably has felt similarly. You don't endure a tragedy and come out of it the same person you were. Physical scars are only part of the change. The mental battle of waking up that first day after an accident and seeing the person you are now, knowing it's not the same as when you went to bed. Your body is different. Some parts scarred beyond recognition. You can't imagine someone else loving this new version of you because you don't love this version of yourself yet.

It's a brutal process.

One that Logan couldn't endure without my help. Just like Halle. "And did you fix his scars?"

I nod, swallowing past a lump in my throat. "But he died under my care."

It feels like someone else says the words as Halle's arms go around my shoulders, her tears wetting my neck. "Oh, Vance. I'm so sorry. No one should have to endure a loss of a friend."

But that's not all of it. "His airway collapsed during recovery. As soon as we gave him something for the pain." My chest feels like ten thousand flames are burning me from the inside out. "Subsequently, he suffered respiratory arrest." My words are flat and clinical. "And no life saving measures could get him back."

Halle's arms tighten around me, and I hope she's understanding why I turned down her case. "The coroner said Logan had undiagnosed sleep apnea. The sedation in the pain medication caused the hypoxia, which ultimately resulted in his death."

In my best friend's death. The man I stayed up all night studying with. The man I stood beside while he married the woman of his dreams.

In one moment, I ruined two lives.

Halle's tears drip down my shirt. "You didn't know."

"It doesn't matter. I was his surgeon. We're the captain of the ship. I ordered the medication. It was my responsibility to ensure his safe recovery." The same thing I told her a few weeks ago.

I take a breath, swallowing down the pain. "I walked away after they administered the medicine. I was on the opposite wing when they called the code, announcing he wasn't breathing, and they needed help. But I was too late."

Pulling back, I push on Halle's shoulders so she'll look at me. "You had the same issue during your last hospital stay."

She shakes her head, slapping my hands away. "My case is different."

"It's not." Does she think I didn't look at her file thoroughly? "Halle, I can't even go into the operating room without my hands shaking and me blacking out. You don't want me as your surgeon."

Wiping the tears from her eyes, she shakes her head defiantly. "Everyone makes mistakes."

I offer her a sad smile. "But mine comes with a lawsuit and an offer of a settlement, requiring the closure of my practice and my license revoked."

I take a deep breath. "My mistake is final."

CHAPTER TWENTY-FOUR

Halle

He believes his mistake is final.

"So, that's all you get? One fuckup?"

Vance turns to me, his eyes seemingly vacant. "My fuckup cost a man his life and a woman, her husband."

But… "It's not like you purposely tried to kill him, Vance. You didn't know about his condition."

Vance stares off behind my head, refusing to look at me. "He trusted me with his life, and I let him down. Now, I can't atone for what happened. My hands tremble, and I black out anytime I get close to the operating room."

He swallows, the lines in his face deepening with pain. "Calista wants to take my license… I'm starting to think that's the best thing I could do for my patients."

I wrap my arms around his shoulders. This man needs a serious hug. "Calista is grieving, but allowing her to take your license in the process would not only be detrimental to you but a tragedy to your patients.

You're the best there is, Dr. Potter. Losing your talent and your passion for helping others would destroy the very people you're trying to help."

Lifting my chin, Vance meets my eyes. "You should never allow another person to destroy your dreams, Peach. Especially not me."

I understand what he's saying. I do. While I know it's insane to give others power over your life, I do. Well, I did.

Caleb, my ex-boyfriend, destroyed my future with one argument, and I let him. For over a year. But then, I placed my happiness, my future, in another—Dr. Potter. I understand Vance would rather me put my hope and dreams in myself. And I am.

I just need Dr. Potter's help to achieve them.

Pulling Vance close, I place a kiss on his lips. "Hope is a dangerous emotion. Sometimes it fulfills us, and sometimes, it kills us. The question is, which side would you rather fight for, because there is no question that you are the hope for your patients, whether you want to be or not.

Vance and I spent the rest of the night locked in each other's arms. We didn't discuss hope or my past or even the lawsuit. Instead, we sought the comfort of one another and the stillness the silence provided. What's more, my hips suffered no pain on the resort's mattress, thanks to Vance stuffing his pillows between my knees.

I thought it was the most chivalrous thing he's ever done until he snatched the pillow from under my head and proceeded to lie on it. I was poised to argue, but then he rolled me over, slipping his arm over my middle, and pulled me into his body.

Dr. Potter and I were spooning.

I don't know if spooning is even the right word. It was like we were one person sharing that pillow. My body was so tight against his that even our breathing felt in sync. I haven't shared a bed with a man. Not since Dickface Caleb. I felt sure I would never be able to fall asleep.

But here I am, with the morning sun streaming through the sheer curtains and my arm tangled inside my doctor's shirt.

"Morning," Vance says with a voice full of gravel and sex.

"Morning." Gah, he's hot when he wakes up—all curls and bed-head. Hopefully, I don't look gremlin-like with tangles and smell like overnight chicken breath.

I remember our food preference conversation. I can't believe Vance doesn't eat chicken. He must be an alien.

"You ready for today?"

Groaning, I pull my hands from his shirt. "Don't remind me—the plane ride home." At least now, though, Vance can use his powers of distraction and send us both back to Texas in better moods.

"No plane ride yet," he clarifies. "I thought we could stay the weekend, and let the Georgia girl see more of Napa."

The idea of spending all day with Vance has my heart beating faster. "I'd like that very much. Thank you, Dr. Potter. You really didn't have to do this."

"I know." A lazy smile pulls up his plump lips. "But what kind of hands-off travel agent would I be if I sent you back home with only views of the hotel room?" He winks, and it's so boyish and playful that I swear my heart utterly melts. "I promised you the full Napa experience, and since my travel agency doesn't offer refunds, we aim for the best review possible."

Oh, he's getting a review. One that includes my lips pressing against his just as soon as I brush my teeth. "You are the sweetest, grouchiest man I've ever met. You know that?"

Vance smirks and that, too, I want to kiss off his face.

"So, where are we going?" I hop out of the bed and enjoy the slow perusal of Vance's gaze before he answers me.

"No questions allowed today."

I think about it for a moment and shrug. "I can handle that."

"Doubtful, but we'll see how long you can last."

I make this ridiculous noise that sounds something like a squeal, and I sprint for the shower. The excitement of venturing around the winery has my body buzzing.

An hour later, Vance and I are cruising down some unknown dirt road in an open-top Jeep. Oak trees loom over us as wayward leaves litter the ground. Despite Vance's instructions, I don't keep my hands inside the car, instead, stretching them out wide into the wind.

It feels like I'm flying, but not in a panicky type of way like when I'm flying in a plane.

"It's right up here," Vance yells over the wind.

I follow his finger to a hidden drive lined with grapevines that span over the hundreds of acres of land. People are weaving between the vines, plucking grapes, and filling the straw baskets hanging on their arms. "This is amazing," I tell Vance, my voice awestruck. "We have orchards back home, but nothing like this."

Parking, Vance grins, a proud smile covering the lower half of his face before he hops out and comes to open my door. "I'm glad you like it."

"Like it?" I gasp. "This place is magical." And I'm probably a little dramatic. "I've lived on a farm my whole life. But dairy farms are much different than vineyards. My eyes wander as I take in all the beauty of nature and grab Vance's hand, letting him lead me to our next stop, which happens to be a fancy building with a woman at the counter.

"Welcome to Vitis Vineyards. Will you be needing a basket?" The woman holds up a woven basket like I'd seen the others carrying and hands it to Vance. "The tour closes at six and the grape stomping at eight. I suggest reserving your spot for the grape stomping first. Those spots book up fast."

I nod at Vance, expressing that we definitely should do it. "We'll take the next available then," he tells her.

The woman prints our tickets, and Vance pockets them before I can ask what time we're supposed to be there. Which would be breaking his no-question rule, anyway.

Instead, Vance takes my hand and leads us down the path between the grapevines. Immediately, I start plucking the grapes and tossing them into the basket on his arm.

"You know," he says, "I used to think this was free labor under the guise of tourism."

I look back, my brows pinched in confusion while he grins, pointing to the grapes in my hand. "You're doing all the picking for them, and what makes it brilliant is you even pay to do it." He shrugs. "It's a genius business strategy."

I can't keep the laugh bottled up. "Stop. Do not even bring that pessimism into my happy bubble right now." Tossing more grapes into the basket, I grin. "It might be ridiculous, but it's not a hospital room or my bedroom. I'm walking on my own without a walker and having a great time doing it."

I realize a moment too late, when Vance's smile falters, that I ended up being the one to bring negativity into our fun outing.

By lunchtime, our basket is overflowing with grapes.

"Are you done now?" It's the same question Vance asked five minutes ago. And unlike last time, I finally give him a different answer. "I think so. My hips are getting sore."

No matter the scenery, the reality is always the same: I will never be able to climb mountains or run miles. But at least I get to explore, and that's all that matters to me—new adventures and new memories.

"How about we grab lunch and rest for a while?"

Honestly, I could use a chair and a glass of water, but I don't want Vance thinking I can't go on the rest of the day. "Sure. If you're hungry, I could eat."

We end up at this cute little café where I shove down all of my food and several bites of Vance's. "This was really good, thank you."

Vance tips his chin like he's too cool to agree with me. "How are you feeling?"

Always the doctor. "I'm feeling like I'm ready to stomp some poor, pitiful grapes."

Vance finally told me that he booked our tickets to the grape stomping at one o'clock. I don't quite know what all is involved in the art of stomping grapes, but I'm excited to find out.

"Are you done picking at your food?" I point to the fish and chips mostly untouched.

"I'm done."

I'm concerned he hasn't eaten and spent most of our time in the café, looking around as if he was waiting on crotch-sniffer to jump out of a bush and slap him again. Which, I wish she would. I'd love to pop her around a little and show her how it feels. It's not like I don't understand what she's going through, I do. But no emotion, not even grief, warrants putting your hands on someone. Especially someone whom you were friends with. Twat-monger—or Calista—whatever her name is, should know that Vance is grieving just as much as she is. Though, I can get rowdy if she decides to put her hands on him again.

"Good." I stand from the table and take Vance's hand. "Let's go stomp out some aggression."

"Will both of you be participating?"

Vance waves a hand at the lady behind the desk, shaking his head. "No, just her."

My eyes shoot up. "You're not going to do WWE Grape Smash with me? I thought we agreed at lunch that we both need to relieve some tension."

He makes a face that says, *does it look like I offer free labor?* "No. *We* did not agree."

Vance hands over the ticket to the woman and ignores my glare. "Give me your shoes and go rinse your feet with the other generous patrons."

Grinning, I slip off my shoes and press them to his chest. "Be careful, Dr. Potter, your uppity is showing."

"My what?"

"Uppity," I clarify. "You refusing to have fun because it's technically making the winery money."

Dr. Potter lifts a brow. "It's not about the free labor but more about the two-thousand-dollar suit I'm wearing."

Have you ever? "Why didn't you wear jeans and a T-shirt?" Who tours a vineyard in a suit anyway?

"I didn't bring other clothes." The way he says it all nonchalant is like he has no idea how pretentious he sounds. But, playing devil's advocate, he wasn't expecting to stay all weekend. For all Vance knew, he was flying here, spending the night, and flying back. No detours through the vineyard.

"Fine. I'll accept that excuse this once. But next time, you're totally stomping grapes with me."

It's then I realize that I basically just admitted I want there to be more dates with Dr. Potter. If you can even call this a date. It's not. Vance is just being sweet and atoning for all the asshole comments and dickish behavior he exhibited the past few weeks. Nothing more.

"The rinse stations are to your left. I'll meet you at the grape tubs."

I don't let Vance's lack of participation stop me from grinning as I rinse my feet, taking his hand as he helps me into the wooden tub full of cool, smooshy grapes.

"Please don't fall, drown, or vomit."

My feet sink down into the grapes, each one popping as I apply more of my weight. "How romantic. Who would have thought the good doctor would have such a plethora of sweet nothings?"

I full-on grin at Vance's scowl and jump. "Ahh! They're squishing between my toes!"

Jumping once again, I slip and stumble to the side of the tub right into my doctor's arms. "Didn't I tell you not to fall?"

I grin up at the man still sporting an epic frown. "I didn't fall. You caught me."

"I see that," he grunts, sliding his hands down to my waist. "I guess if I want to keep the lawsuit count to a minimum, I'll have to keep my hands on you."

Placing my hands on his shoulders, I lean in, placing my lips over his. "I think I want more than just your hands on me, Dr. Potter."

CHAPTER TWENTY-FIVE

Vance

I cast a cursory look at Halle, my gaze unwittingly traveling lazily down her body. "You're filthy," I muse.

Acting on my reaction to seeing Halle dirty and covered in grape sediment would be a terrible decision—but I think I've established I don't make great decisions where Halle is concerned.

But her fucking smile and sharp wit seal my fate as she strides up to me and cups me through my pants. "And you're hard, Dr. Potter. What shall we do about that?"

I'm thinking tossing her face down on the mattress and spanking her bare ass sounds good right about now.

"Do you find me being messy attractive?" she whispers, her lips brushing mine. "I think you do." She squeezes my biceps, kneading the tension there before moving to my chest and unbuttoning my coat, slipping her hands underneath my jacket. "You like my chaos, don't you?"

My breathing increases as she toys with the buttons on my shirt.

"Come on, Vance, be dirty with me." With a simple swipe of her hand, she smears the residue down my chest, staining my clothes.

"Look at that." She grins. "Now, you're filthy, too."

A man can only be pushed so far before he snaps, and my band of restraint has been pulled entirely too tight for too long.

In one fluid motion, I scoop Halle into my arms and toss her onto the bed, her tits bouncing as she hits the mattress with a gasp.

She knew what she was doing, breaking me down day by day.

It was only a matter of time before I broke.

And now she has to pay—there's no layaway option here, either.

"Spread your fucking legs," I bark, unbuttoning my shirt and shrugging it off as I put a knee onto the bed, my predatory gaze on her body, hungry for something wholly chaotic.

"Ask me nicely."

I pause, noting the pink on her cheeks, and smirk. "Ms. Belle, *please* spread your fucking legs, or I'll flip you over and show you how I handle disobedience *out* of the office."

A hesitant grin is the only thing she offers me.

Message received, Ms. Belle.

Grabbing Halle's ankles, I yank her to the edge of the bed, reveling in her sudden gasp. "You see, Ms. Belle," I mind her hips and flip her over so she's face down on the mattress. "No one defies me in the office—" I push her dress up over her hips and place a kiss on the cotton underwear I'm about to ruin, "—or out."

The sound of ripping fabric is so satisfying that I moan when her bare ass cheeks come into view.

"Oh, Peach. I can't wait to see this ass turn pink."

Halle lifts her hips, giving me permission and silently agreeing that she's had this coming. All the push and pull between us is finally getting resolved. She's made my cock hard so many times by mouthing off, telling me I'm not her boss.

But here, right now, she'll have no doubt as to who owns her.

"Tell me, Peach. Do you enjoy disobeying me?" I skim her back, dragging my lips across her heated skin until I reach her firm, rounded cheeks.

"Yes," she whispers, my eyes closing in satisfaction as I place a kiss to her ass.

"Is this what you wanted?" I tease her, settling my palm against her bottom. "To see me come undone?"

Another, "Yes," is all I need to lift my hand, my palm coming down on her bare cheek. The smacking sound sends a rush of euphoria through me as I raise my hand again and repeat the motion.

Halle's skin pinkens and goosebumps break out onto her back. "You doing okay, Peach?"

Pain may be connected to pleasure, but I never want to confuse the two. Spanking should be enjoyed by both parties.

Halle turns her face, holding my gaze. "Do it again."

So, I do, until I turn her bare ass a beautiful shade of pink. By the fourth slap, she's panting, and I've run out of patience. "On your knees."

I lift Halle's hips, keeping her knees comfortable on the mattress while getting her ass high in the air. "Don't move," I tell her, enjoying the view of my patient, legs spread, her body half-covered to tease me while I lower behind her, my fingers spreading her ass cheeks. "I'm going to kiss you here," I tell her, slipping my finger between her folds, "And you're going to respond with only 'yes, sir.'"

The time for sass is gone.

"Do I make myself clear?"

Halle's back arches as I drag my finger in and out, spreading her wetness around. "Yes, sir." She moans between short pants.

"Good girl," I praise, wasting no more time with instructions, lowering my head and pressing my lips to her warm, soaked flesh.

Both of us moan at the contact as I push my tongue into her center. She bucks at the intrusion, and I pull back. "Didn't I tell you to stay still?" I scold.

She doesn't even bother lying. "You'll have to hold me, the sensation is—"

175

I need nothing more. My hands go to her hips as I tilt them upward, burying my face in her pussy once more.

"Oh, shit," Halle moans, tugging at the sheets and urging my tongue deeper, rougher. The taste of her arousal is like top-shelf bourbon—sweet and intoxicating as the tension coils in my core while I fuck her with my tongue.

I've wanted to bury myself inside Halle since I stretched her the first time. Her bare pussy, peeking out of my shirt as she moaned, had me fighting for my spot in Heaven.

"Vance," she cries out, "you have to stop. I'm about to come."

And she thinks that's a solid reason for me to remove my tongue from her pussy?

I think not.

Instead of answering her, I place a gentle kiss to her clit and pull away, my face wet with her arousal and turn to lie on my back, lowering her over my face.

"Oh, fuck!"

I nip at her clit for swearing and suck hard, enjoying her returning whimper when I push two fingers inside her, pumping them furiously while my free arm holds her close, forcing her to feel every ounce of me.

Her body begins to tremble. She's close, and when I add another finger, she explodes around me. "How you doing, Peach?" I ease in and out of her until the tremors subside.

"Pretty freaking amazing, Dr. Potter." She laughs, and I roll her over onto her side.

"I'm not finished with you yet," I tell her, standing up.

"I sure hope not." Her gaze goes to my cock, straining against my pants, begging to come out. "Otherwise, I fear for the safety of the people at this resort."

She's hilarious but not wrong.

"Oh, trust me, the only one who should be concerned for their safety right now is you." I'm going to fuck this woman into the mattress.

She grins as I stack pillows in two rows of two. "I'm not scared of you, Vance."

"You should be."

"But I'm not, and there's nothing you can do about it."

Clearly. Halle has never backed down. Not when I was rude and certainly not when I told her no. It's the main reason my dick and I are having problems walking away from her now. It's why I continued to make up excuses to see her again. Picking her up for work... Taking her home... Making sure no other surgeon touched her...

I'm addicted to Ms. Belle, and I can't explain why.

At first, I thought it was because she had shown me an act of kindness when I blacked out in the bathroom, but I'm not sure that was the start of my infatuation with Halle. To be honest, I think I was intrigued the minute she walked into my office and asked me about layaway. Like I wasn't a world-renowned surgeon. Like I was just another doctor. Nothing special. Nothing noteworthy.

The weight of Logan's death and his wife's subsequent lawsuit had me second-guessing clinical decisions so much that the pressure of being a surgeon developed into a debilitating disease. And then, this sassy, southern belle comes into the mix and makes me feel like I'm back in med school with no expectations or legacies to live up to. To her, I'm just another face in the crowd.

"Come here." I hold out my hand and beckon Halle forward.

She sits up, her excited smile beaming as she crawls to me on the bed until she reaches the end. "Now what, Dr. Potter?"

I finger her dress. "Take this off."

I want to see *all* of her.

"As you wish." She shimmies the fabric up and off her shoulders, her tits bare underneath as she finds my gaze on her breasts.

"A bra didn't work with this outfit?"

Why does the thought of anyone possibly getting a peek at her hardened nipples through the thin fabric make me want to rage?

Reaching out, I roll the hardened bud between my fingers. "Do you do that a lot?"

Do I need a policy requiring bras?

She leans forward pressing her lips against mine, and I waste no time drawing her closer, parting her lips with my tongue and kissing her roughly before pulling back. "We're gonna discuss this later."

I can't wait another second to be inside her.

"Whatever you say, Dr. Potter. You're the boss." She flashes me a wink. "At least to most people."

Before another smart-ass comment can come out of her mouth, I scoop her up wedding-style and carry her to the other side of the bed, laying her on her side between the pillows, which I rearrange behind her back and under her head and hip. "Don't even think of moving."

I'm liable to lose my shit completely as pent-up as I am.

It takes me a matter of seconds to shuck off the rest of my clothes and crawl across the bed to where Halle awaits, naked and flushed, while her wide eyes sweep along my body.

"You really should eat more chicken, Dr. Potter. It would do wonders for that whole six-pack abs thing you have going on."

I tip her chin, lying down next to her. "I'll keep that in mind."

Right after I come inside her—fuck. "I don't have a condom." Unlike Astor, I don't come to these conferences with the intention of getting laid. I haven't needed a condom in a very long time.

Halle pauses. "Surely, you're clean, right? Being a doctor and all…"

I grin. "Being clean has nothing to do with being a doctor, but yes, I'm clean."

But I'm in no need of a baby right now. My life is far too fucked up as it is.

"I'm on birth control," she says, moving her hand to palm my face.

I nod, not bothering to continue the conversation that is already a boner-killer. Instead, I scoot in closer and thread my legs between hers. "Is this comfortable?" With a total hip replacement, I want to be mindful of the position I put her in. On her side has the least impact.

She trails a finger down my abs, cresting over the smattering of dark hair until she finds my cock, sliding her thumb over the tip and smearing the liquid there. "I'm more than comfortable, Dr. Potter."

Her hand grips me, and with a steady up and down motion, my head bows forward. I take a peaked bud in my mouth, sucking eagerly

178

as I find her cunt and slip two fingers inside. She's dripping wet. "Guide me in."

I can barely get the words out when Halle positions me at her entrance. Every muscle in my body is coiled with tension as we both take a breath, waiting for me to push inside her.

One second. Two—

With her leg, Halle pulls me by the ass, shoving me inside. Both of us groan as she stretches around me.

"Oh, gosh," Halle moans, "this is sooo not bad dick."

Inhaling, I choke, her random outburst catching me off guard. "You were expecting bad?"

She shakes her head, a faint smile appearing. "I wasn't expecting such… fullness."

I'm not sure if she means physically or metaphorically, but I decide now isn't the time to wonder. Ms. Belle's body molds to mine like it was always meant to as I push in all the way, shushing her cries with kisses as I thrust over and over until my body is met with a familiar tingle.

"Look at me," she cries.

I'm panting, holding back, my neck straining as I try looking away. Everything is too intimate. Too real. I'm not supposed to be looking at Halle, making love to her as we face each other with our bodies intertwined and connected.

This was supposed to be a release.

A bandage for the ache.

But now, as she holds my face, with our noses pressed together, I let her watch as she tears down the barrier between us, her body taking my demons and burying them inside.

CHAPTER TWENTY-SIX

Vance

I can't sleep.

Even with Halle's naked body pressed against mine, her breathing a sweet, rhythmic lullaby against my chest, I couldn't stay in bed.

I made love to her.

I've never shared intimacy with another person, not like I just did with Halle. She broke a dam that I didn't know I had built, and now, I can't rebuild it fast enough to stop the thoughts swirling in my head.

Memories I don't want to remember.

Like Logan's death.

Calista thought I had a lot of nerve showing my face at a medical conference for physicians who save lives.

She claimed I wasn't one of those people anymore.

I'm a murderer, just as she declared before slapping me.

The sting to my cheek was nothing like the stab to my chest her words provided. I grieve Logan just as much as she does. He was just as much my brother as Duke and Astor, and now, he's gone. The pain of losing someone isn't something I can fix or refine. These scars go far too deep.

I will wear them for all eternity.

But the thing I can't yet accept is the punishment for my failure. I failed Logan and Calista. She's right, I don't deserve to practice medicine anymore. But what about those patients like Halle? Sure, there're other surgeons who will take her case, but will they heal the scars below the surface?

For some reason, Halle doesn't want another surgeon. She wants me, and while I've tried everything I can think of to get her to change her mind, she won't. I've simply only been able to delay her by setting an expectation she won't be able to meet.

Halle has no one here in Texas to help her with postoperative care.

Except, she could use the teenager at the motel.

Or my brothers.

Either of them would agree to help just to see me in the operating room again.

But why?

Why make Halle suffer by using a surgeon who should have handed over his medical license after he killed his best friend?

Halle deserves me whole and unjaded from past failures.

Not this shell of man who can't even walk into his OR without vomiting. Calista was right, I'll only destroy more lives. And I can't do that to Halle. Her light is so pure, so resilient, so—

The door to the balcony slides open. "What are you doing out here?"

Halle is wrapped in a sheet, her legs bare as she turns on the light, stepping out into the cool air. "Can't sleep?"

Everything about her is untainted by the adversity in her life. With her concerned frown and bright eyes, she walks over to me, sitting in the rocking chair, and lifts my chin. "What's going on in that head of yours, Dr. Potter?"

Nothing.

Everything.

You.

I settle for a lie. "I'm enjoying the peace."

She makes this tittering noise that says she believes me as much as she believes in the Easter Bunny. "You're having a pity party is what you're having."

She flops down on my thighs, kicking her legs over the armrest and adjusting the sheet back over her body before snuggling into my chest. "Okay, now you can resume your party. I'll just be here, sleeping."

Closing her eyes, she rests her head on my chest, her arms looping around my neck as I begin rocking again. We stay that way, with her cradled in my arms, as the sun peeks up from the rolling hills of the vineyards, peacefully rocking in silence until she breaks it.

"I told myself a long time ago that I would never put my faith in people." She never looks up. Instead, she holds on to me tighter, keeping her gaze between our bodies. "People are broken and tainted by circumstances. They will let you down, and after Caleb, I couldn't afford to ever allow that to happen again."

She inhales, and I want to stop her right here. I know the story between her and her ex, Caleb. It was hard enough to read, let alone hear. But like my therapist says, talking about pain leads to healing. I haven't quite come to that part of the process, but who am I to deny Halle hers? For all I know, this moment of voicing her pain into the hills she called magical could be what she needs to move on.

"But I was wrong. If we can't put our faith in others, then how can we have faith in ourselves?"

"We don't."

Sometimes, there is no hope to be found. Calista has no hope of ever getting her husband back. I have no hope that I will ever recover from his death. Hope has no place in some people.

Halle pats my arms like I need to brace myself. "But we do. You just have to find it. Like I did."

She takes a breath, settling in my arms. "I was fourteen when I knew I was going to marry Caleb Conrad." She laughs, but it lacks humor. "Small towns sometimes breed small dreams. And the only dream I had was to marry the mechanic's son. Caleb was smart, charming, and hardworking. Everything my daddy said I would be lucky to find in a man. But it was all a lie."

I pull the sheet tighter over her legs as if it alone will soothe the ache as she relives this part of her life she wants desperately to forget. After all, he's the reason for her scars.

"Caleb promised we'd get married right after college. He would become a successful businessman while I landed the role of a lifetime. We'd travel the globe and see every landmark this world had to offer. Our dreams were only four years out of our reach."

Pulling her hand from my neck, she swipes under her eyes. "Four years and a substance abuse problem." If I didn't think I could feel any shittier in the wee hours of the morning, I was wrong. Halle's sniffles absolutely gut me. "College wasn't like our small town, where nothing happened—you were right about that." She chuckles, and it makes me want to take back every shitty thing I said to her in the beginning. "College had parties, pills, and freedom. And Caleb wanted it all. He stopped coming over. Stopped calling. He stopped everything that had to do with me."

"And sobriety, apparently," I can't help from blurting. I hate this fucker, purely based on the pain he caused this woman.

"Yes, but I had made a commitment, and I couldn't let Caleb go down this path without a friend. Both of us went to college on a scholarship. My parents owned a dairy farm, and when my father had his stroke, it was too much for my mother to keep up. They sold all the cattle and moved in with my aunt and uncle, just so they could pay for the rest of my college.

"You see, my parents were forty-three when I was born. They'd tried so hard to have a baby for years and were never successful until my mom thought she'd had a virus that wouldn't go away. They've always worried they wouldn't see me marry or meet their grandchildren. So, they were excited to know that Caleb and I were planning to marry so soon."

Smoothing a hand over her hair, I brush it behind her ear. "They wanted to give you everything."

She nods, a sweet smile emerging. "They did, and all I could think was I would one day pay them back when I landed the role of a lifetime. I would buy them a small farmhouse, like they loved, but would only stock the land with enough cattle for them to be pets."

She swallows. "And then I got the frantic call from Caleb's friend that changed my entire life."

My arms tighten around her. This part of the story, I know all too well. "Caleb was trying to drive home from a party. His friend—I can't even remember his name—didn't know what all Caleb had taken, just that he was panicked and acting erratically."

The pictures of her body... God. Just remembering the graphic images in her chart where her bones protruded from her skin has me sick to my stomach.

"I rushed to the party and found Caleb in his old pickup, surrounded by several guys, all trying to convince him to get out."

Her hand trembles against me, and I grab it, pressing it to my lips.

"We argued. I opened the door." Her voice hitches. "I tried to pull him out..." She hiccups, fighting off the tears. "Someone tried to pull me back, but I stumbled."

And he floored it, crushing her body underneath.

Lifting her closer, I pull her to my chest, shushing her softly. Some things you can't unsee. Having this veracious woman telling the story without hate is so much worse.

"He didn't know what he was doing. He didn't mean to hit me."

But he did, and from what her chart says, he spent the next eighteen months in rehab while she went through a total hip replacement, rods in her thighs, and an infection that set her back months.

"I don't even remember the pain. I just remember thinking that I hope someone stopped him before he hurt himself."

I wish he would have, but lucky ol' Caleb came out of that night with nothing but a headache.

"I remember the ambulance... and the helicopter. But it wasn't until I woke up, covered in bandages, that the pain hit. I couldn't walk. My legs looked like they'd been through a meat grinder. And my boyfriend... was gone. I remember thinking I would never walk again. My parents didn't have the money for all the therapy I needed. They didn't even have the physical strength to help me from the bed to the bathroom when I was discharged."

I unintentionally rock us faster. The thought of Halle helpless and alone while she fought through the pain in a body that no longer felt like hers has me ready to sprint from this vineyard and up to that piece of shit's door. How dare he cause her so much pain and not atone?

"My aunt and uncle were very kind and allowed me to move in with them, too. But the recovery—wetting myself when I couldn't get to the bedside commode—was humiliating. I remember lying in bed crying as my aunt, who I didn't really know, cleaned up after me, and thinking *is this what the rest of my life looks like?* I knew I would regain my strength eventually, but at the time, in the moment of feeling like a burden, you don't really turn to logic."

Her story is starting to sound like my therapy sessions—except, with a brutal example.

"And then I saw that woman's story. The one I told you about."

She looks up at me with a tear-soaked face but the most perfect smile. "I knew that if she could overcome, then so could I. You may not be a Marvel hero, but a potter sounded pretty perfect to me."

She deserves that man, that *potter*, as she calls me, not this one. "Did the motherfuc—Caleb ever apologize?"

Or let you get a few hits in with a bat?

She shakes her head, her smile still firmly in place as she reaches up and pushes at my lips, attempting to make me smile. "Nope. And while that bothered me for a while, I learned to get over it."

I scoff. "You don't get over something like that."

"You can; all you have to do is forgive." She shrugs like it's so fucking simple. Like you can erase years' worth of pain with one simple action.

"And how did you forgive him?"

"It's not like there's a magic button," she says, choking on a laugh. "Forgiveness is a choice. One that I constantly need to remind myself of. Caleb making a mistake does not make him a bad person or an unforgivable one. As you're aware, we all make mistakes, Dr. Potter. If we were only able to make one mistake in our lifetime, with no one to forgive us and allow second chances, we'd be lonely, fucked-up messes. We'd have no reason to live. No reason to try again or do better. I decided that I was wasting years feeling sorry for myself and holding on to my hate for Caleb. He messed up, sure. But so have I."

"I highly doubt you've ever done something so horrific."

She shrugs. "Not yet, but that doesn't mean I won't. But at least I rest in the knowledge there are people out there like me, who will forgive and give me hope that I can try again and be a better person."

"Do you think Caleb is a better person?"

"I don't know." She pulls at my neck, and I meet her halfway, placing a kiss to her lips. "But I know that despite your tragedy, *you* are a good person, Dr. Potter. And it's people like you that give me hope that one day, Caleb will be, too."

CHAPTER TWENTY-SEVEN

Vance

"Sometimes, I still call him a dickhead, but he's a forgiven dickhead at least."

Her words, as the sun came up with her wrapped in my arms, still linger with me a week later. Will Calista ever feel like Halle does? Will she ever find it in her heart to forgive me? Better yet, will I ever find it in my heart to forgive myself?

Halle said it was a choice, a constant decision she must remind herself to make.

Is that what I need to do in order to move on from this?

Do I deserve another chance to help patients like Halle?

I want to.

I do.

But with each passing second of this conversation, that hope is dwindling.

"Vance, are you listening to me?"

I cast a look up at Astor. "I heard you. We were fifteen grand short last month."

"Yes!" He looks exasperated already. "Because you haven't performed a surgery in a year!"

Astor paces around my office, tugging at his tie. "I thought you would be able to put this behind you. I thought the therapist was helping."

He thought wrong.

"Relax, I'm getting back into the operating room next week." I promised Halle a fresh start; it's time I delivered on that promise. Though, it doesn't make it any easier going back into a room where my life was completely destroyed.

Astor stops, realization sinking in. "Who?"

I swirl the bourbon in my glass. "You know who."

"Halle," he breathes, nodding like we can all handle this. "Duke and I will be in there with you."

I don't say no.

"We'll run over the procedure notes together so there won't be any surprises," he continues, his mind shifting into surgeon-mode. "Nothing will happen to her. We'll make sure of it."

Two years ago, I would have punched my brother in the face for acting like I even needed his or Duke's help in the operating room. Frankly, it's a giant fucking insult to suggest I need their supervision. "Thanks. I'm sure Halle will feel better with you both there."

I would too, but I'd never admit it to Astor. He's already more worried about my mental health than he should be.

"Do you have an exact day next week?"

I shake my head. "No, I need to talk to Halle—make sure she's ready."

Astor nods. "She's more than ready, but let me know when you decide, and I'll make sure my schedule is clear."

I should be grateful I have such thoughtful brothers, but the panic of going back to the operating room and slicing open a woman that has become more than a friend, overwhelms me. "Appreciate it. Now, if you'll excuse me, I need to get to a meeting."

I stand up and make my way to the door, ignoring Astor's watchful eye. "See you tonight at the gym?" I need someone to beat some sense or calmness into me. I'll take either at this point.

"Yeah, sure, but Vance—"

"See you at seven then."

I slam the door, cutting off any more heart-to-heart discussions he might be contemplating and walk down the hall to the surgical suites.

I don't know at what point I decided that now was the time to face my demons, but I do know that it's Halle's fault.

Sitting with her on the balcony of our room, watching the sun come up while she spoke of forgiveness and hard work to get where she's at, I couldn't imagine making her suffer one more moment without giving her what she desired—what she deserved.

A fresh start.

A new beginning.

Even if it comes at the expense of knowing that my time with her will come to an end. But that was always the case. Halle was never supposed to make a career out of being Astor's secretary. She wants more for her parents—herself—and she deserves it.

I just wish she had a better surgeon than me. Someone who doesn't vomit at the sight of the double doors and scrub sinks.

Logan might have died in the recovery room, but the operating room was the catalyst—at least that's what Dr. Johnson, my therapist, claims. But this room, the one that I've entered thousands of times, full of arrogance and demands, is now full of pain and humility as it reminds me that no one can play God, not even me.

The operating room humbled me.

It brought me to my knees with the pain of a thousand mistakes all in a matter of a few hours.

Had I been more prepared, more thoughtful in Logan's case, things might have turned out differently. And now, Halle is stuck with a surgeon she thinks is worthy of giving her the new life she deserves.

I've never felt like an imposter until now.

She'd be better off with Duke or Astor, yet she won't even discuss it. After our time together in Napa, she's been even more determined to see this plan of hers through. She's missed so much in her life. The simplest pleasures have been taken from her, and she, understandably, wants them back.

At the end of the hall, the doors to the OR stand between me and Halle's future.

It's just a room, Vance. It's just like an exam room—sterile, cold, and familiar.

And haunting.

My heart pounds against my chest, and my breathing turns shallow as I approach. I was wrong; I can't do this. I'll black out before I even walk through the doors. Stopping, I lean against the wall, trying to catch my breath.

But I'm unable to. I can already feel the unconsciousness creeping in It won't be long before it consumes me. Halle has to understand that she can't stay here forever. She wants to move on, and I'm the only one standing in her way.

"Vance?"

Oh, fuck.

I pinch my eyes shut and slide down the wall. "I'm okay."

I can feel the heat of her body before her hand slides in mine, a quiet comfort as she just sits there, not saying anything else.

Hours could have passed, but I'm thinking it was more like minutes, when I finally realize my breathing has normalized, and my heart doesn't feel like it's slamming against my rib cage.

"It's been a long time since I've seen the inside of an operating room," she finally says.

I grunt. "If you weren't so stubborn, I'd never let you see the inside of another one. You don't need the scar revision, Peach."

You're perfect exactly as you are.

"It's not about the scars anymore, Dr. Potter."

I pry open my eyes and turn my head to the side, finding her piercing gaze full of fearless determination. "It's about finishing what I started. The scars might have given me the excuse to change my life by setting goals to put me on the path to my dreams, but over the years, I've learned that the scars don't define me, only I can do that. This scar revision is an end to who I was and the beginning of who I am now and who I will continue to be. By doing my revision, you're offering me closure. You're erasing all the reasons to look back on who I used to be. I don't want to remember what happened, just what I learned from that incident."

Her free hand comes to rest on my cheek. "I'm not asking you to change me, I'm asking you to allow my body to serve as a reminder that I made it. I didn't break. I didn't quit. I endured, and I came out the other side more beautiful than I ever imagined."

She gives me a smile that, if she hadn't been successful in breaking me before, would have obliterated me with the mere sight. "I'm asking you to finish this for me. Close the last of my wounds with your hands."

"What if I can't?" My heart has picked back up with its racing pace.

"You can. I believe in you."

I close my eyes, fighting the urge to be an asshole and push her away. I want to give her what she needs, but I'm not sure that I can.

"I can't even go into the room, Peach."

It's something I've never admitted to anyone but Dr. Johnson.

"Have you tried to go in with a friend?"

My eyes fly open as she stands, tugging on my hand. "No."

I don't think I can stand seeing Halle in the operating room, her skin sliced open, tubes down her throat...

"Then, I say we start desensitizing you to the idea of me naked in the OR."

"What?"

She drops my hand and looks past me down the hall before offering me a sly smile. "If you're struggling with seeing my naked body on the table, it might be best to get you used to the idea."

I didn't realize I said the words aloud. I'm losing my fucking mind.

Especially when Halle tosses her shirt at my feet, her baby pink bra a soft contrast to her milky skin.

"Come here, Dr. Potter."

She beckons me with a crook of her finger, and everything south of my belt hardens despite where she's headed. All I can think of is her naked body as she straddled me in that chair on the deck, rocking her hips back and forth on my cock in a sweet, laborious torture as she drew out my pleasure by controlling me with her body.

And here she is again, using my need for her to lure me to the depths of hell, where my demons await.

"The longer you take, the more naked I'll get in the hallway," she threatens as I take a hesitant step closer. Thankfully, this particular OR is mine. Potter's Plastics has a total of three ORs that my brothers and I share. Sometimes, we use each other's rooms if something is broken in one of the others, but it's not often. So, I only feel a mild sense of panic that one of my brothers will come down this hall right now and see Halle's naked body.

Still, I'm not going to risk it.

Eating up the last steps between us, I snag Halle by the waist, pulling her flush against my body. "You're not playing fair, Ms. Belle. Let me remind you of my thinning patience."

The smirk I remember seeing wrapped around my cock in Napa is my undoing, and I push Halle through the double doors, greeting my demons for the first time in a year.

CHAPTER TWENTY-EIGHT

Vance

The antiseptic smell stops me as soon as we get inside.

"Keep going," Halle begs, sliding the coat off my shoulders and taking my hand. She places my palm on her chest, skimming it flat against her body until coming to a stop at her waist. "Unbutton my pants, Dr. Potter."

The trembling in my hands and the urge to flee is strong. "Feel my heart, Dr. Potter."

Halle moves my hand back up to her chest, the steady beat of her heart rhythmic and calm. "I love the operating room. Do you know that?"

I shake my head.

"After the accident, I struggled being around people. The scars. The questions. The pitiful looks… I couldn't get past the fact that I would never be the same. I would always be the woman who was run over by her boyfriend. At one point, the rumors evolved, and I became the woman who was beaten by her boyfriend and tried to commit suicide after a bad breakup by jumping from an overpass.

"The point is, no matter what happened to me in the operating room, I was always the same. A patient. And the people in this room were the same. The doctors and nurses who cared for my injuries were my heroes. There was no judgment. No rumors. Just anonymity."

Halle's heart beats steady under my palm, and I find myself pulling in a deep breath and exhaling just as her hands come up and cup my cheeks. "In this room, Vance, you are the same person. You are one of the best surgeons in the country. The past doesn't matter. Neither do the events that led to your scars. In here—" She drags a hand down to my heart and presses down. "In the OR, you are *the Dr. Potter.*"

Standing on her tiptoes, she moves her hand and presses a kiss over my heart. "You don't have to let Logan's death rule you, Vance. The OR has no place for the past—only the future."

Her gaze tracks down to my hand, resting comfortably against her skin. "You create futures, Dr. Potter. Don't let your scars take the freedom of this room from you or your patients."

Her words are full of such conviction that I find myself taking a step toward her, walking her backward and farther into the room. "You sound like you really believe that, Peach."

She presses a chaste kiss to my lips. "And you sound skeptical, Dr. Potter."

Skeptical? No. Intrigued? Yes. "You think the anonymity of this room is the solution to my... issues?"

I don't need to clarify I'm talking about the blackouts and tremors in my hands. Halle has seen me at my worst, enough to know what my issues are.

"I think changing the memory you associate with this room to something different will help your focus and bring you back to a place of anonymity."

I don't know that her theory will actually work, but having her naked in what was once my kingdom is rather... provocative. She's right; in this room, I am *the Dr. Potter.* I'm the king of this palace. And my queen... is offering her submission, here in the sanctity of my throne room.

"Well, Ms. Belle." I press my hips against hers, allowing her to see the power she's giving back to me with just her faith. "In my operating room, everyone follows my commands."

Her head falls back with a moan as I press a kiss to her neck. "Yes, Dr. Potter…"

But then, she turns toward my face, her voice a naughty whisper as she comes back with, "Whatever you need to hear to get hard."

The look she shoots me is lethal—infused with lust, acceptance, and pure sass.

And I plan to fuck it from her face and enjoy every second of it.

Twisting Halle's hair in my hand, I tug her head forward so I can stare into her eyes when I put an end to her quips for the day. "I'm gonna fuck that smart mouth until your eyes water."

With my free hand, I reach around her back and unclasp her bra one-handed, watching as the pink material flutters to the floor between us.

Halle's throat bobs as she chances a look down, my cock straining against my pants. "Looks like the tremors have subsided."

That they have.

Halle's presence has an uncanny effect on my body.

She's the calm to my chaos.

The salve to my burn.

And yet, I am none of those things for her.

Because I let the scars change me.

I let the demons win.

But I can end that here.

I can be her potter.

Threading my hands through her silky hair, I tip her head back, pressing a kiss and swiping my tongue over the seam of her lips until she parts them on an exhale. "Good girl," I praise, breathing against her mouth before filling it with my tongue. I take my time, nipping and exploring every facet of Halle Belle as her body relaxes into mine.

It doesn't feel like we're in the operating room—more like in my bedroom, safe, comfortable, and away from the noise of the world.

Comfortable.

What a strange feeling for me.

When was the last time I have been so comfortable with someone who wasn't my brother?

"Vance." Halle pulls away, her hands going to my belt, undoing it. "You said you were going to fuc—"

I cover her mouth, tsking. "No profanity out of that sweet mouth of yours."

Not that I don't enjoy a nice vulgar sparring with her, but not right now.

Now, I want to see her put my cock between her lips and look up at me with those big, cerulean eyes. "Get on your knees, Ms. Belle."

Lowering, Halle's eyes sparkle with something like delight as she pulls me free, fisting my cock, giving it a few pumps before guiding it to the back of her throat.

The first swipe of her tongue is a jolt of pure pleasure as it sends me bowing forward. Grabbing the OR table for support only spurs Halle on as she grabs my ass and pulls me in deeper, controlling me—loving me with the sweet pulls of her mouth.

It's then I know that I'm completely and utterly fucked when it comes to this woman.

"That's enough," I bark out, already guiding her up to her feet.

She takes a moment before wiping her mouth off with the back of her hand and grinning. "What's wrong, Dr. Potter?"

"What's wrong?" I drag my fingertips along her perfect tits, circling her pink nipple until her head rolls back. "What's wrong, Ms. Belle, is that you have far too much control in my domain." In one motion, I lift her by the ass and sit her on the table. "Lie back." I push gently on her chest, reveling in her excited pants as her back arches against the cool metal.

Leaning over her body, I drag my lips across her nipple, my breathing making it hard. "You're on my table, Peach. Is it everything you dreamed of?"

She moans, her hands going to my head, holding my mouth to her breast. "Better than I imagined."

Oh, she hasn't seen anything yet.

With a parting kiss, I pull her hands from my hair and place them up by her head. "Grab the back of the table if you need to, but don't move until I say you can."

This moment, with Halle laid before me, is the most sensual thing I've ever experienced. She's exposed, beautifully vulnerable and exceedingly brave, as I love her through the fog of my demons on the very table that birthed them into existence.

My fingers play at the button of her pants, skimming the soft skin at the waist. "I want you bare—I want to fucking feast on you."

"Yes," she moans, reaching behind her for the edge of the table.

I chuckle. Smart girl.

Flipping the button open, I unzip Halle's pants and slide them down her legs. I kiss each calf before I take her legs in my hands, bending her knees, and placing her feet on the edge of the table.

"Remember," I warn her, leaning down and using my shoulder to open her legs so I can settle between them, "no moving."

I don't give her time to acknowledge her understanding. I simply can't wait any longer to devour the woman who dared to come between me and my demons.

As soon as my tongue parts her sweet flesh, Halle's back bows off the table, her whimpering urging me deeper as I nip at the hot bundle of nerves.

"You're moving."

And I don't give two shits. I just want to see her squirm as she holds on to the table, biting her lip to keep from crying out as I push two fingers inside her. "Are you ready for my cock, Ms. Belle?"

I fucking hope so. I don't know that I can wait.

"I'm ready for you to fuck me, Dr. Potter, and stop being a cock tease."

My fingers stop their thrusting.

Did she just suggest I was a cock tease?

"Vance?" She tries sitting up, and I push her back down. "Are you serious right now? Are you stopping?"

Oh, no. I'm not stopping.

Withdrawing my fingers, I step back and send Halle a smirk from across the table. "You better hold on, Peach. I don't plan on stopping again."

I press the button on the side of the table, lowering it until Halle's pretty cunt is lined up with my cock. "No matter what—" I step between her legs and place a kiss to her knees, "—I'll never look at this table the same way again."

I'll forever envision Halle's naked body—a lamb before the slaughter.

"Thank you for trusting me." I kiss her other knee. "For continuing to have faith in me when I had lost it."

I don't know that this one event with Ms. Belle will suddenly change the relationship I have with the OR or my ability to perform surgeries in it. What it does mean is there's hope. If I can love Halle in a place of pain, then there's hope I can love being a surgeon again.

Halle's hand finds mine as she interlaces our fingers. "You were always the potter. You just needed to be reminded."

Reminded.

She's the only one brave enough to *remind* me of anything, let alone argue until I believe it.

I never thought of myself as a potter, but now, locking eyes with a woman who truly believes I am one, I want nothing more than to become that for her.

Swallowing a knot of emotion, I step forward, aligning my cock with her center, and push in slowly, her breath hitching as her pussy stretches around me, molding to my cock like a second skin.

"Vance." She squeezes my hand as I pull out and plunge deep inside her. Those perfect tits of hers bounce with each push of my hips. Our bodies collide over and over, faster and faster, until I'm feverish, never getting deep enough.

This woman is my salvation—no, this woman is *my* potter.

She took the broken pieces of me, and here, on this very table, she pieced together something wholly beautiful between us.

Halle sat with me in the dark, burning bright, even after I tried smothering her light.

I don't deserve this second chance.

This unrelenting faith she has in me.

But when she calls out my name, breaking apart before me, I realize I'll do anything to repay this woman so she can stand anew in the light she never let die.

CHAPTER TWENTY-NINE

Halle

Six weeks later...

"Holy shit! I've never seen a surgical cap look so hot."

Up until now, Vance has been completely silent, pacing back and forth in front of the window of the pre-op room, where I'm currently being poked and prepared for surgery. "Don't fucking start, Duke. I'll have you escorted out."

I send Duke an apologetic smile, but he just laughs it off. Vance's mood, while edgy, is still okay. Which is a good sign. For the past six weeks, Vance and I have spent most of the day in the operating room. Banging. Eating. Talking. Anything that helped make the operating room feel more familiar and relaxed.

He has acclimated so well with this approach, his therapist agreed that he was finally ready to perform surgeries again. Vance, on the other hand, wasn't so excited. Especially, since I was to be patient zero.

But he had to get back to performing surgeries.

He now associated the operating room with good memories of me naked. It only made sense.

Vance didn't think so.

But like every other time we've disagreed, I didn't let up. Vance was performing this surgery for both of our sakes.

Still didn't mean he was happy about it or that I didn't hear him puking in the bathroom this morning, but he's doing it, and that's all that matters.

Watching this man battle his demons has been nothing short of soul-crushing.

But his therapist says he's ready.

He no longer shakes.

He hasn't blacked out since that first time I found him in the bathroom.

He can do this.

I have faith in him.

"Are we ready, Dr. Potter?"

Astor pops his head through the door and gives me a thumbs-up, ignoring Vance's glare.

"I know I'm ready," I say with enthusiasm. I've tried very hard not to show even a hint of anxiety regarding this procedure. Vance has been watching me so closely that I knew if I showed any signs of doubt, he would call the whole thing off. And we are so not doing that.

"Good," Astor says, coming over to my bedside and taking my hand. He places a kiss to the top of it, where a clear bandage covers my IV. "I'm going to take you down to the OR and get you ready."

"No," Vance clips out. "I'll take her."

Astor keeps his eyes on me when he says, "I don't think that's a good idea, brother. You're already on edge. Seeing the anesthesiologist give her the medicine could be a trigger."

Honestly, I want Vance to do what he feels like he needs to do to get through this, but I understand Astor trying to separate our personal relationship. It's probably best Vance treats me like any other patient.

Straightening, Vance strides up to the bed, his eyes hard and full of authority. "Astor, your involvement in this case is a courtesy. You will not question me in my operating room."

I smother a gasp while Astor fights off a grin. "Whatever you say, Dr. Potter. It's your case."

And that's how I find myself being wheeled down the hall with all three Potter brothers at my side.

When the anesthesiologist places a mask over my face a few minutes later, and asks me to count backwards… I fall asleep to a pair of green eyes.

My potter has arrived.

It's funny how the best things in life bring you pain before they bring you pleasure.

I knew going under the knife again would be excruciating, but unlike the last time I found myself waking up in a recovery room, I welcomed the pain.

"How are you feeling?" I fight through the fog of anesthesia and turn my head, finding the source of the whispered question. Duke.

"Hi," I say, testing the heaviness of my tongue. "How is he?"

His mouth, shaped similarly to his brother's, tips up into a smile. "You've just been gutted and stitched back together, and you're worried about how Vance feels?"

Vance.

He says his name as if he's a guy we know who shops at a retail market and not the man whose brilliance surpasses that of a mere mortal.

"Yeah," I croak, my voice raspy from the tube that was in my throat. "I need to know if he…"

I need to know if I brought back his trauma.

Duke tucks the blanket at my side and sighs, pointing to the foot of my bed, where an exhausted Vance sits, his hand resting on my foot as he sleeps.

Grinning, I look up at Duke. "He's not sitting in a pile of destruction."

"Nor did his hands shake once while he was operating."

Relief blooms in my chest, sending a rush of endorphins through me as I focus on the man at my bedside, beautifully broken and incredibly strong. "He did it," I whisper to Duke. "He overcame his demons."

Duke chuckles. "I wouldn't mention that to him. He wasn't happy about it."

That doesn't concern me. "When is he ever happy?"

"True." Duke laughs, standing and checking a few of the monitors at my side, his tone turning serious. This is the Dr. Duke I've never seen before. "Are you in pain?"

With a quick mental scan of my muscles, I flex, noting tightness and an ache I know will turn into a fiery pain later. "Nothing I can't handle."

"That's not what he asked you." My gaze whips to the man at my feet, lifting off the bed and coming to stand next to his brother, his hair mussed from sleep as he looks at the monitors for himself.

Duke flashes me a wink. "Now that Dr. Dreamy is awake, I'll leave you in his grumpy hands." He steps back and points at me. "Astor doesn't want to see you at the office for six weeks, Hal. Doctor's orders."

"Eight weeks," Vance barks out. "She needs to heal properly."

My ass. "Tell Astor I'll see him in six," I clip out, ignoring Vance's twitching jaw and narrowed gaze. I don't need him adding two weeks just because he's overbearing and paranoid. This isn't my first time recovering from a surgery. I know exactly how much time my body needs, and six weeks is more than enough.

"Right." Duke grins, backing away slowly. "Well, just remember to bring a clearance letter from your doctor."

My heart sinks as the two brothers smile, their expressions eerily similar to one another.

"Sorry, Hal. Your doctor always overrides your boss."

I turn and face a smug Vance. "How convenient."

"It can be."

He thinks this is funny, and while I would love to argue with him,

I don't want him to drop his smile. Who would have thought I would have received this reaction from Vance after surgery? I was completely prepared for Duke to tend to my post-op care while he made excuses as to where Vance was.

Duke pauses at the door. "Be a sweet boy, Vance," he says and then grins at me. "Don't kill him until I can help you hide the body. I don't want you lifting over five pounds and popping stitches."

I bark out a laugh and immediately regret it when a sharp pain shoots up one side of my body.

"Duke!" Vance barks, his earlier smile falling into a tight frown as he lifts one side of the blankets, checking my incisions.

"I'll come by your place later," Duke promises, ignoring Vance, "and feed you and Oscar."

The blanket crumples between Vance's fist. "No need. She'll be at my place."

I swear Duke's inhale is as sharp as mine as we both stare incredulously at Vance.

"I'm sorry. Did you say *your* house?" I ask, since clearly, I'm on good pain meds that cause hallucinations.

Vance nods tightly. "I told you I was not discharging you to that shithole with only a fish to take care of you."

My stomach dips, and I'm pretty sure it's not from the meds. "I don't recall that clause being in the consent form I signed." I dare him to lie.

His mouth tightens. "And I don't recall giving a fuck."

As Duke disappears, I watch as Vance busies himself with checking the monitors and adjusting settings that are more than likely unnecessary before I grab his hand. "Hey."

His gaze whips to mine, sure and steady, with a focus I've never seen from him before. "I'm fine. Maybe you should go rest. You look tired."

And cranky, but I don't say that aloud since I would rather stay on his good side. No doubt the surgery took an emotional toll on him.

"I'm not tired," he lies, casually pulling his hand away.

"Okay," I drawl. "Maybe you should go have a drink then. Celebrate a successful surgery?"

He doesn't even take a breath. "No."

Okaaay. I see this line of suggestions is going nowhere fast.

"What about your afternoon patients?" Surely his whole day isn't blocked off for this?

"My afternoon is clear, and you should probably rest."

Translation: Stop asking him questions and suggesting he leave. Clearly, he's staying. "Are you in pain?" he finally asks, his voice low and careful.

"No. I don't want any IV pain meds." The last thing I want is for Vance to relive his trauma by sedating me with medication and worrying if I'll code like Logan. I can't undo all the progress he's made. Besides, the pain is bearable right now.

"Don't lie. Tell me if you're in pain." He takes my hand, squeezing it. "I can handle it, I promise."

He's totally lying, but I appreciate the attempt he's making. It means he's over the hump. My potter is molding his broken pieces into something wholly beautiful.

I flash him what I'm sure is a drugged smile. "Tell me, how hot did you make me? I don't want to make Serena feel bad when I come back to work."

A rare and unfiltered smile crosses Vance's face. "First, Serena was never in your fishbowl when it came to beauty."

Does anyone else find it absolutely adorable that he just used a fishbowl metaphor?

"Second, you are no more beautiful now than you were going in."

My heart flutters, and I hope the monitors don't pick it up. "Why would you say that?"

Not that I wanted to look like Kylie Jenner coming off the operating table, but I expected improvement. "What the hell did I pay you for then?" Part of me is joking, and the other part of me wishes I didn't have bandages and tubes so I could beg him to get naked with me. I'm sure that scandal would give the office water cooler some business.

Vance fiddles with the blanket, tucking it gently under my arms. "Nothing I could ever do would make you more beautiful to me." A faint blush appears on his cheeks, and I somehow manage not to ask him to marry me. I'm kidding. But tell that to my heart and the steady thump humming under my ribs.

We want this man.

Every. Broken. Piece.

"Besides," Vance grins, "you never paid me."

That's true. "Shit. Run back to my office and grab my purse."

"You better not be walking around with stacks of cash in your purse." He lifts a brow, daring me to confirm it.

"How else am I supposed to get it to you? I meant to give it to you yesterday when we were going over the pre-op stuff and signing the consent forms, but I forgot. I was a little excited."

Okay, I was a lot excited.

My dream was coming true, and the man I lo—respect—agreed to face his demons and perform it, even though I heard him throwing up all morning in "his" bathroom before I went in, wiped his face, handed him a mint, and walked with him, hand in hand, to the surgical suites.

I knew Dr. Potter was a hero. He just needed to remember that the tears in his cape didn't render it useless.

Vance clears his throat, pulling my attention back to him. "I don't want your money, Peach."

What? "Why not?"

He shrugs.

"Oh, no, you don't. You acted all shitty about my layaway comment. You're taking my money."

If you look in the dictionary under the word stubborn, you'll find this man's picture.

Have mercy on my soul.

"I don't have to do anything, Peach." He flashes this boyish smile that seriously needs kissing. "Perks of being the boss."

He leans down and kisses the top of my hand. "Use the money to chase your dreams—" He swallows, suddenly looking uncomfortable. "Or whatever you want. You have a fresh start now."

A fresh start.

It's what I wanted.

A new beginning.

The opportunity to pursue my dream of acting. Buy a house for my parents. Maybe a bigger fishbowl for Oscar.

It's what I've lived for all these years, and yet, somehow, I don't feel as happy as I thought I would.

I find Vance's eyes, heavy and tired. "Lie down with me?"

He shakes his head. "You need your rest."

"I'll rest. Just lie with me."

If this is the end of mine and Vance's relationship, then I want to savor every moment I have left with him.

"Halle." He sighs, running his hands through his hair. "I don't want to hurt you."

But he will.

No matter if he lies next to me or not. I've fallen for the grumpy surgeon, and in a matter of weeks, he'll expect me to move on, just like I wanted.

This is him making sure my recovery is uneventful.

This is him making amends.

He's atoning, forgiving himself for Logan's death.

Staying here would only complicate his recovery.

And as selfish as I'd like to be and tell him how I feel, I care about him too much. I want to see the Dr. Potter I saw on TV come back. So, I'll cherish these last weeks with him, and then I'll let him go. It's the least I can do for him. He's done so much for me.

"Please," my voice cracks as I reach my hands out to him one last time, for one more favor, "don't make me beg."

Vance blinks slowly as if he realizes this is the beginning of the end. "We'll go home in a few hours," he says instead, and I'm almost disappointed until I see him slip off his shoes and put his phone on the table. "Tell me you understand, Halle."

I nod. "We're going home."

At least for the next six weeks.

CHAPTER THIRTY

Vance

"Come here and taste this."

I toss my keys on the table next to the door and pad my way into the kitchen where my patient is sitting on the counter in my worn-out Harvard shirt. "Please tell me you have underwear on under there this time."

She licks the red sauce off her finger before crooking it, beckoning me closer. "I'm thinking you should know the answer to that question by now."

No is the answer.

In the past five weeks since Halle has been recovering at my house, she's effectively domesticated me.

I don't hate it.

Every evening, after my last patient or surgery, I come home to find Halle half-naked in my clothes. Dinner is usually cooking on the stove while she dances around, singing Disney showtunes to Oscar while he swims in my crystal vase.

"Did you have a bad day at the office?"

I take a step closer, pushing between her knees, careful to mind the new skin that's almost healed, and ignore her question, choosing to ask one of my own. "Astor tells me you've been scheduling his appointments." I arch a brow, daring her to deny it.

"Astor is shitty at keeping secrets," she returns with a grin. "Open." She dips her finger back into the spaghetti sauce and holds it at my lips until I open, taking extra care to suck the sauce off harder and more thoroughly than necessary.

I have missed her, even though I spent the entire car ride home fuming that she defied me by forwarding her work phone to her cell, answering Astor's calls and scheduling his appointments, when I haven't released her back to work yet.

Astor thought I knew.

He thought wrong.

Ms. Belle has become quite clever these last five weeks, figuring out how she can defy my orders. She already convinced me to agree to a six-week recovery period instead of eight. I put nothing past her when it comes to getting what she wants.

Releasing her finger, I slip my arms around her hips and pull her to the edge of the counter. "What am I going to do with you?"

"Fuck me against this counter?"

I press a kiss to her mouth, my tongue slipping in as soon as she takes a breath. "I'm thinking that sounds like too pleasurable of a punishment."

She leans in, nuzzling my neck. "The worst kind."

Damn, I've missed this woman, and I've only been away from her for ten hours.

Time seems to tick by slower without her presence in the office.

Though, since I performed her surgery, I've been busier than I have in years. I owe many patients their time in the OR, and thanks to Halle, they are finally getting it.

Taking care of Halle these past few weeks has been like watching a wrecking ball tear down the walls around me.

She's changed how I see myself as a surgeon.

As a man.

And as a brother.

My therapist called it a breakthrough.

I call her an angel.

Halle is the reason I've spent so much time at the office, rebuilding myself—my practice. I needed to make up for the pain and lost time I've spent wrestling with my demons.

"Vance…" Halle's sing-song voice interrupts my thoughts. "Are you all right? Did something happen at the office today?"

Yeah, I didn't get to strip her naked on one of many solid surfaces.

I didn't get to talk to her over lunch.

I didn't get to smell her hair as I buried my face into her neck, kissing every inch of bare skin I could reach.

Yeah, a lot of things happened today, but none of them were what I really wanted—to be here, with her. Taking the first week off after Halle's surgery radically changed how I wanted my days to go.

It started with eating her pussy before breakfast.

Lunch came with sucking her tits on the island.

And dinner, well, that routine hasn't changed.

"Nothing happened at the office," I tell her, tugging off her T-shirt and tossing it to the floor. "I arrived, spent the whole day in the operating room, and then I came home—to you."

The best fucking part of my day.

I can't even remember what it felt like to come home to an empty house and a bottle of bourbon.

Halle's legs wrap around me and pull me closer. "How many lives did you change today?"

She's asking how many surgeries I performed. It's the same question she asks every day, and every day that I answer, it puts a smile on her face that I never want to see fade. "Four."

I kiss up her neck, lingering at her earlobe.

"And how did it make you feel helping those four patients?"

My kisses trail lower and down her chest, heading for her nipple. "Uncomfortable."

Every day, she hopes for a different answer, and every day, she gets the same one. Trust me, I want to feel different. I want to walk out of that operating room feeling changed and whole, but the fact is, with Calista's lawsuit still ongoing, her accusations still staring at me when I open an email from my attorney, I can't help the nagging fear that creeps back in. At any moment, I could fuck up and unintentionally harm a patient.

I could change their lives in a way they never imagined.

Just like I did Logan and Calista's.

Doing more surgeries hasn't changed that fact.

What has changed, though, is coming home to someone so full of life that it completely distracts me from the present chaos.

"I'm ready to stretch early tonight," I say, swiping my tongue across her nipple before pulling it into my mouth, taking a leisurely suck.

Her back arches as her hands go to my hair. "What about dinner?"

I lift her off the counter and turn off the stove. "We'll reheat it. I need to take care of you first."

Halle chuckles. "How very considerate of you—taking care of me after a long day at work."

Kneeling on the Italian rug in the living room, I place her on her back, admiring the sparkle in her eyes. "It's part of your recovery process. We can't skip a night."

I grin, parting her legs and lowering to her center like I wanted to do the first night we found ourselves in this same position—the night I craved to stretch her pussy first.

"I've waited all day for this," I admit, a groan slipping out the moment my lips meet her flesh, wet and dripping just for me. The taste of her desire chases away the demons better than any bourbon could.

"Oh, shit." Halle tries wiggling away from my pulls on her clit, but I'm ready, lowering my shoulders and pinning her hands to the floor.

"If you can't stay still, then I can't stretch you properly," I chide.

I can certainly make her come with my tongue, but she likes riding my fingers just as much as my face.

Her voice is whiny when she stops tugging against me, inhaling a breath. "Fine, but remember, Dr. Potter, you're not the boss all the time."

Meaning: When she's on her knees, she can bring me to mine. She's the only woman who's been able to take control away from me.

And I don't mind—not at all.

At her admission, I let go of her wrists and push two fingers inside her, reminding her that right now, she's the one laid out before me, on her back, and at my mercy. Pressing a kiss to the top of her hip, where I refined one of the scars, I look up to find her eyes. "Are you happy, Peach?"

I don't know if I'm asking if she's happy with me or with her new, refined scars. Both answers hold my attention equally.

She takes my free hand and slips my index finger in her mouth. "More than I've ever been."

And right now, that's all that matters.

She's happy.

I'm happy.

At least until Friday, when I have to face Calista at the deposition regarding Logan's death.

Just thinking about it has me losing rhythm, and Halle doesn't miss it. "Stay with me, Vance," she pants out, squeezing my hand. "Feel me." She pulls my hand, stretching my arm up her chest to her heart. "Feel all of me."

With her heart beating faster than usual, I focus on its steadiness as her pussy grips my fingers. She's right, I am here. With her.

And, right now, as her sweet cunt spasms around my finger, that's enough.

"I hope you brushed your teeth."

I pause towel-drying my hair and arch a brow at the naked woman in my bed. "Come again?"

She grins, getting up, her tits bouncing with the motion, and grabs my hand. "I'm just saying pussy and garlic spaghetti is a bad combination."

"We've crossed a line with this conversation." I shake my head, letting her pull me onto the bed.

"Don't be embarrassed, Vance. Even esteemed doctors can have bad breath. It's nothing to ashamed of." She takes the towel from me and looks longingly at my dick that she rode on the bathroom counter prior to my shower, which is where she had to come up with this whole bad breath thing.

I narrow my eyes. "I brushed my teeth—prior to you sucking me off, actually."

We're seriously having a bad breath discussion.

"I'm teasing." She pops me with the towel before climbing on the bed and settling onto my lap, facing me. "But seriously, are you ever insecure?" She places the towel on my head and takes over drying my hair, which feels absolutely incredible.

"I get insecure," I tell her. "Clearly, you've witnessed a few of those moments."

"I mean with your body." Her tone lowers, and I think I know where this line of questioning is going.

"Most of my scars are on the inside." I can hear her disappointed exhale. "But there was this one time, in med school..." I pull the towel away and toss it on the floor. "I was drunk and thought my scalpel was a straw." I flash her a wink. "One of those rich-people-metal-ones."

She laughs.

"It wasn't until I dropped it on my bare foot, that I realized it was my scalpel I left lying out on the dresser when I was practicing cuts on fruit." I hold my foot up, letting her get an up close and personal view of the jagged scar that nearly cost me a pinky toe. "Eight stitches and a never-ending ribbing from Astor later, I have a nasty scar that prevents me from ever wearing another pair of flip-flops."

At closer inspection, Halle throws her head back and laughs a deep belly sound. "You're full of shit. You've never worn flip-flops."

This woman…

"I'll have you know, I was much cooler in college."

"I highly doubt that." She lets out another chuckle. "Dr. Potter would never be caught in anything other than expensive loafers."

"I wear tennis shoes in the operating room," I correct her. "It's better for my knees."

And back, but that's not the point.

"Why not have the scar fixed if it bothers you?"

And this is what she really wants. Validation.

"Do you think because you had scars revised that you're somehow less of a woman than the people who live with their scars?"

She doesn't respond, and I take that to mean yes.

I sigh. "The scars will always be there, Peach. It doesn't matter how small or noticeable they are. The fact is, they are part of us. But that doesn't mean we have to allow others to have the knowledge they exist. Scars are the windows to our past. No one is entitled to that experience. So, I leave the scar on my foot because it's a scar I don't mind revisiting, though it still makes me self-conscious of the way my foot looks in a pair of flip-flops."

I chuckle, hoping I don't fuck up what I'm trying to say.

"But the deep scars… the ones inside that I don't want anyone to see… those have only been opened for one person, and she managed to refine them into something manageable."

I kiss the side of her face, tasting salty tears. "Never feel like you're less for managing the memories. You didn't let them manage you. You survived, Peach, and the world is a better place for it."

I pause, swallowing. "I am a better man because of it."

CHAPTER THIRTY-ONE

Halle

I knew Friday would be a tough day for Vance.

Which is why I made sure I loved him into the wee hours of the morning. I wanted to consume every bit of energy and anxiety he had. What he needed was a clear head and room for focus.

No blackouts.

No tremors.

What happened with Logan needed to be told with grace and humility, not with misery and regret. Though Vance feels both of those emotions, it's important for Calista to see that Logan's death was not Vance's fault. As Logan's surgeon, Vance did everything he could to save his friend. Unfortunately, Logan suffered a tragic outcome.

Life isn't always fair.

It wasn't for Logan, Calista, *or* Vance.

With death, you never move on, but you can move forward and learn to live with the pain and absence of a loved one.

That's what I hope today will bring Vance and Calista—closure.

Now, though, as I roll over to an empty side of the bed, where Vance should be this morning, I'm not hopeful.

For all the strides he's made since I've been here, I'm afraid reliving the nightmare of the day he lost Logan will set him back. Vance doesn't deserve that kind of hell. Not now. Not when he's worked so hard to get back into the operating room—to take back his life.

I can't let him lose everything he's built these past weeks, and I certainly can't let him face Calista without backup. The last time he saw her, she slapped him. That's not happening today. The only one who can slap Dr. Potter is me—and I prefer slapping his ass, not that pretty face. Dr. Potter has become more to me than just my surgeon.

He's my friend, one who spends time with me, plays games, and participates in the very trendy exercise routine of naked yoga. But more than being my friend, Vance has become my protector—always making sure I'm safe and cared for when he's here or away at the office.

And then there's this little thing called love.

I love Dr. Potter and more than just as a doctor.

I've grown to love Vance's domineering ways, with his rare shows of sarcasm and fun.

Vance is complicated and deep, yet he has a softer, more fun side that hardly anyone gets to see.

But he showed it to me.

He might not use the L-word to describe our relationship, but I can tell he feels something for me. The speeches… the rare shows of vulnerability and openness… Vance has a heart, and it very much likes me.

Does it like me enough to keep me here in Texas with him?

I don't know.

Do I *want* to stay in Texas?

I didn't come here with the intention of falling in love and making a new home in Bloomfield. I came here for a surgery to fade the memories that held me back from taking the career I wanted in show business.

Vance gave me the fresh start I asked for.

Am I ready to put those dreams on the back burner because my heart has chosen someone to kick off this new life with?

Maybe.

I don't know. This isn't something Vance and I have discussed. We don't throw around the L-word or mention future plans other than dinner. But he's had to have thought about it, right? What happens in a few days, when my recovery is over? Does he expect me to pack up my clothes and Oscar and head back to Clyde's with Remington? Or do I live here now? It's all so confusing and terribly selfish to even think about, when Vance is going through hell today.

Get your priorities straight, Halle. You aren't going through mental anguish by reliving a friend's death and having attorneys ask you why you didn't know your friend had sleep apnea?

Gah, I've wasted so much time just sitting here.

I need to find Vance.

Vance didn't answer his phone.

No surprise there.

But, at least, Astor did. Apparently, they met at the gym early this morning to spar or beat the hell out of each other, and Vance was so preoccupied, he left his phone there.

Astor grabbed it, but by the time he made it out to the parking lot, Vance was gone.

He never made it to the office, which is where I am heading to join in the search for him.

"There she is!" Astor greets me at the door, wrapping me in a big hug. "I can't believe my brother forgot to lock you up today. What's it been—a week since I last saw you?"

It has, but that's not the concern here. "Have you heard from him?"

Astor doesn't seem as worried as I think he should be, considering his brother disappeared a couple of hours ago.

"Duke found him at the cemetery, where Logan is buried."

A sudden ache spreads throughout my chest. How terrible he must feel to have gone to the cemetery. "Is he okay?"

Astor guides us down the hall toward our offices. "Duke's sitting with him. He hasn't said anything yet."

Oh, my gosh. "I should go to him."

Astor opens the door to my office. "Let's see if he can work it out. Duke is there just in case."

Just in case he runs? Has a blackout?

"Why don't you help me with the patients we have backing up out front? Serena called out sick, and Autumn could use the help. We can reschedule Duke's patients for her. Vance only has one consult today. I don't know if we should reschedule her or wait to see if she shows. It's later in the afternoon, before the…"

Deposition.

Why would Vance schedule a consult on the day he was supposed to give his deposition?

I nod slowly, chewing my lip so I don't burst into tears. This patient must really mean a lot to Vance for him to see her today.

He won't reschedule her. I know it. He'll show up for this consult.

Straightening, I inhale and flash Astor a go-getter smile. "So, how many patients do you have?"

At least he has the nerve to look ashamed, lowering his eyes and fighting back a grin. "I might have overbooked a little bit."

"Of course, you did." I shake my head and walk into my office, stowing my purse in the desk. Really, I could use a distraction from worrying about Vance. Like Astor said, Duke is with him. He'll make sure he returns to me safely. "All right then, let's get these patients taken care of."

Astor and I haven't stopped working in five hours. It's been a whirlwind of rescheduling, apologizing, and escorting patients into exam rooms.

My feet are tired, I'm hungry, and am still very much concerned about Vance, who still hasn't shown up this afternoon.

"Excuse me."

Looking up from the stack of papers on the counter, I find a woman, likely in her early fifties, with a soft smile. "Yes, ma'am. How can I help you?"

"My daughter has an appointment with Dr. Potter at three o'clock. Charlotte Adams. She's on her way. We drove separately."

So, this is Vance's consult, the one he'll see on one of the worst days of his life.

"Ah, yes," I confirm, double-checking Vance's calendar. "Dr. Potter is running behind. Let me show you to the waiting room and grab you a refreshment while you wait."

Where is Vance, and why hasn't he called? He could use Duke's phone. This behavior is not like the man who called me hourly when I was at his house recuperating.

A sinking feeling settles in my stomach.

Maybe now that I'm healed, and his duty as my surgeon is done, he's moved on.

Maybe Mrs. Adams's daughter is his next project?

No, I won't think like that. Vance is a brilliant and caring surgeon. He treats all his patients with the same respect and kindness as he did me.

He just needs time to get himself together for the deposition.

That's all.

"Thank you, sweetheart." Mrs. Adams walks toward the open waiting room, and I rush out from behind the desk to meet her.

"Let me show you where we stash the best sodas."

Which is in the same location as the other sodas, but thankfully, Mrs. Adams accepts my overhelpfulness, walking alongside me to the waiting room and allowing me to pour her a drink as she takes a seat in one of the oversized chairs.

"Here you are." I pass her the plastic cup and settle in the chair beside her. Call me nosy, but I'd love to know what this woman and her daughter's story is. Vance accepted their appointment for a reason. I'd like to know why.

"Thank you, dear. You're very sweet."

I lean back in my chair and smile. "Is this your daughter's first appointment at Potter's Plastics?"

Mrs. Adams nods. "Yes. I'm only here for moral support, though. I feel a little weird being here."

"Not all plastic surgery has to do with facelifts and butt implants." I chuckle.

If Caleb had never caused my accident, I would have continued to always associate plastic surgery with boobs and cheek implants.

"Well, when you're my age, you really don't worry about scars."

I frown. "So, why is your daughter meeting with Dr. Potter?"

A smile widens across her face as she speaks. "She's going to her first prom in the spring."

"Aww. How fun."

She nods. "It can be… for some girls. For others, like my daughter, it's a *monumental* event. One that she wants to be absolutely perfect. You see, Charlotte has been homeschooled for the past several years since she developed End Stage Renal Disease from her long-term battle with diabetes."

My breath hitches.

"The doctors assured us that a kidney transplant would save her life, and it did. I was a match, and after months of recovery, Charlotte is back in school and attending her first prom."

"And you want Dr. Potter to smooth the scars from the transplant?"

Mrs. Adams sighs. "The surgery wasn't without complications, unfortunately. Charlotte ended up with an infection that required two additional surgeries to debride the wound."

I fill in the rest. "And now, all that's left of her former life is a scar."

Mrs. Adams nods. "One that she wants removed so she can wear the gown of her dreams."

Tears sting the back of my eyes. "I completely understand."

"Oh, you do?" Mrs. Adams seems shocked.

"Dr. Potter recently revised some scars for me. It was something I had wanted for a very long time."

"And did it make you feel better?" She shakes her head. "Don't answer that. I'm sorry. I just worry about my daughter's confidence. If I'm doing the right thing by bringing her here."

Taking her hand, I squeeze. "The right thing isn't always clear, but in my opinion, you can't go wrong with following your heart."

I wipe away a tear as my statement hits me straight in the chest. *Follow my heart.*

Is that what I want to do? Stay here with Vance instead of head to California?

Before I can truly consider the thought, my phone buzzes in my pocket. "Excuse me," I tell Mrs. Adams, thinking it could be Vance finally calling.

I stand, already walking away when I answer. "Hello, Vance?"

"We did it, Hal! You have an audition!"

Kristen's voice immediately has me sighing. "Hi, Kristen." I try to force some enthusiasm into the call, but it comes out sounding more tired than anything.

"Uh, hello. Are you serious right now, Hal? I call and tell you to pack your bags, that I scored you an audition, and you answer me like a depressed chipmunk. What's going on? I thought you would be happy now that you're days away from being released with your hot new body!"

Kristen has a way of making people think she's downed gallons of caffeine when she's on the phone. Her voice is always high-pitched, and she spits out her sentences at lightning speed.

"I am happy!" I lie, this time faking it a little better. "You just caught me at a weird time." Which is completely true. "When's the audition?"

"That's more like it! The audition is set for Tuesday at 2:00 pm."

The door to the office opens, and I expect Astor's next patient.

Instead, I'm met with the angry eyes of Dr. Potter. "Uh, I gotta go, Kristen. Text me the details."

Hanging up—I'll apologize to Kristen later—I hurry to catch Vance, when Duke grabs my arm and pulls me to a halt. "Don't. Just let him go."

Turns out, Duke was being literal.

CHAPTER THIRTY-TWO

Vance

"Are you going to tell me how the deposition went, or should I just wait for you to get drunker and blurt it out?"

I lift the glass of bourbon to my lips and down the rest of the glass in front of Astor, who decided to barge into my office like an inconsiderate asshole. "If I'd wanted a babysitter, I would have asked for one with tits."

Astor lets out this whistle that, if I were sober, would be annoying. "The mouth on you tonight… good thing I had Duke take Halle home. Otherwise, she might come to her senses and leave your pathetic ass."

I laugh out a bitter sound. "Halle's come to the end of her recovery. She doesn't need another excuse to leave me. Our relationship is done."

Even if it wasn't, if Halle ever found out what was said at today's deposition, she'd leave me without hesitation. Suspecting you love a monster is different from *knowing* you love a monster. Who am I kidding? Halle doesn't love me. All of this—the job, the surgery, the recovery—was all so she could move on with her life. She never planned on staying in Texas. I'm merely a pitstop on the road to a new her.

"Vance."

Astor lets out a deep groan that, if I didn't know him better, would make me think he's tired. But Astor is rarely tired. He survives on little sleep.

"Let me help you. Let me be your big brother here."

Standing, I pour another glass of bourbon. I don't bother with the two-finger shit. I want a whole fucking glass. "I don't need a big brother right now, Astor. Go home."

"I'm not going home until you tell me what happened at the deposition that put you in this state."

My "*state*," as he calls it, is another glass of bourbon away from being shitfaced. "You're smarter than this, Astor. Clearly, the deposition went swimmingly." I hold up the glass, indicating I'm being completely sarcastic.

"What happened? Did Calista say anything to you?"

I shake my head. "Worse, she cried—couldn't even stay to hear me finish."

It was a memory I will never get over. My best friend's wife looked as if she could vomit right there on the conference table, shaking her head as I went through Logan's record, staying professional and answering only the questions asked by Calista's attorney. Richard advised me to stick to the facts and keep my eyes from drifting to Calista.

I lasted an hour before I looked over, saw her sobbing silently, and got up. Richard tried to stop me, but all I could see was her and Logan, gathered around the bar in my basement, drinking, laughing, and talking about the old times in college. I couldn't stand the sight of her just sitting there, breaking down with no one to comfort her.

But it wasn't my comfort she wanted.

I get that.

She wanted Logan back.

"She said she'd wished it would have been me who died," I admit to Astor. "I agreed."

Astor springs from the chair, his emotions not dulled by the alcohol like mine. "Fuck, Vance! Don't say that. Logan dying was tragic, it was. But you've seen death before, brother. We're doctors; we see death."

"When was the last time you had a patient die?" I challenge, watching as his face falls. "That's what I thought. You haven't. So, you can't tell me you wouldn't feel the same way. Logan was like a brother to me."

Astor comes to stand in front of me, snatching the glass from my hand. "Then, as a brother, you should know how it feels when one thinks that he deserves to die because of an event he couldn't control."

"But I *could* control it!" I jump up, meeting my brother chest to chest.

"No, you couldn't! You like control, Vance. I get that. But, brother, you have to accept that you have none. Control is a figment of your imagination. Just like perfection, it can never be achieved."

I try pushing away, but Astor downs the last of my bourbon and shoves me instead. "Logan's death was not your fault."

"You don't know what the fuck you're talking about." I sit down, my eyes suddenly heavy.

"I know that you're destroying your own life to atone for something you had no control over."

"Go to hell, Astor." I'm so over this conversation. All I want is for this lawsuit to be over. Richard seems to think the deposition went down beautifully. I showed concern by attempting to comfort Calista—apparently, a jury eats that up. But I don't care what the jury thinks. It won't change the fact that I lost two people who were like family to me.

"Get up. I'm taking you home. Maybe Halle can talk some fucking sense into you. I'm done."

"Thank fuck. I didn't ask for your mommy wisdom." I really deserve to be punched.

Astor chuckles. "Well, someone has to be the one to tell you how stupid you're being."

Stupid.

Richard said something similar today. "Richard doesn't think we should offer Calista a settlement." Closing my eyes, I let my head fall back to my shoulders. "This is where you offer up that mommy advice of yours."

Even I felt bad when I said the words. I'm being a monster dick, and I can't seem to stop. I just want the pain to end.

I hear the breath Astor releases. "Man, I don't know. On one hand, you didn't do anything wrong, on the other, Calista won't drop the suit. Dragging either of you through a trial will be messy. We all saw what happened today with a deposition just down the hall in our conference room. I can't imagine the state we'll get you back in after a trial, when Calista's attorney goes after your sunshine-filled personality."

I raise my middle finger and flip him off.

"I don't say this often, little brother, but I agree. Settle this case. If you don't, I'm afraid there will be nothing left of you."

Halle's asleep when I get home.

That fact should have been comfort enough.

But it wasn't.

Our relationship has always been about helping one another through tough times. Tonight, as she hears me stumble through the front door, is no different.

"Hey," she says on yawn. "I tried waiting up for you."

I move through the room, bypassing the bed altogether, and head toward the bathroom. "You shouldn't have."

Before coming home, Astor and I went to the gym, where he let me get a few hits in before he kicked my ass bloody. I felt better, but no less sober, thanks to bottle of bourbon I took with me. I might have made it through the deposition, but I have no doubt that the pain is just beginning.

I need it all to be finished.

Halle.

Calista.

The lawsuit.

My job.

Everything.

I just want it gone.

"Okay, rude." She sits up in bed in her favorite pajamas—my Harvard T-shirt—and eyes me closely as I stumble through the threshold. "Great, you're drunk again."

"The fact that this surprises you, impresses me."

Just call me Dick Potter.

Halle shakes her head, getting out of bed and coming to my side, finally noticing the red welts on my face. "What happened to you?"

I knock her hand away. "Astor thought I was being a little too mouthy."

The softness in her voice gives me pause. "Come to bed with me. We'll talk about it in the morning." She intertwines her fingers in mine, and all I can feel is the comfort she'll take from me soon, when she leaves for California.

"Don't," I tell her, pulling away and backing into the bathroom. "Don't act like we're some kind of couple."

Halle jerks back like I pushed her. "You should probably stop before I add to Astor's welts."

She should probably get in her licks now; she won't have another chance after tonight.

"I gave Astor your return-to-work papers—that's if you still need a job now that you're healed." I dare her to argue her intentions.

"That's not fair. You knew why I came here. I never kept it a secret from any of you. Heck, Astor is the one who *offered* me the job! I was happy bagging groceries!"

I take another step back, creating much-needed distance between us. "Well, now you can go back to being happy. My commitment in seeing you through this recovery is done."

A tear streaks down her face, and I have to quell the urge to reach out and wipe it away. "What are you saying, Vance? That our relationship was only about the surgery?"

No. "Yes."

I just want to rip it off like a Band-Aid.

"Yes?" Her lip trembles in the bathroom light, and it takes everything in me to stand there like an asshole and deny what she means to me.

"Yes. You came here for a surgery, Ms. Belle, and I provided it—with great results, I must say." If being an asshole were a sport, I'd hold the world record. "With that little need out of the way, I'm not sure what else I can help you with."

I didn't see her slap coming, but I wholeheartedly deserved it. "You're a bastard."

I nod, not bothering to acknowledge the hit to the cheek. "You knew this when you met me."

"You're right, I did," she agrees, wiping angrily at the tears.

That's it, Peach, fight for the future you deserve. One without a man who will drag you down with him.

"I thought..." She sniffles, and it sends an ache through my chest.

"You thought what? That a few great days and a fabulous blow job would suddenly make me a better man?"

Please, baby, just go. Don't make me keep breaking your heart.

"No, people don't change overnight. I, for one, know that. I was just hoping you were changing." She scoffs. "Clearly, I was fucking wrong."

I let her have the F-word this time. After all, she could have said much worse, and I would have deserved it.

"So, we're done here?"

My heart can't take any more, not while she's crying, looking like I betrayed her in the worst way.

And I have.

Halle Belle deserves so much better. Now, she can lump me in with that dickbag who ran her over in the first place. It's safer for her to get away from me—from any man who can't give her the fucking world.

"Okay, Dr. Potter." She nods, forcing a smile like the brave woman she is. "I understand."

What's left of my soul crumbles.

Goodbye, Vance. You're dead to her now. Great fucking job.

"Good," I clip. "I'm glad you understand."

She backs away. "I do. I understand you're a coward."

She's not wrong.

"You're a coward that I hope wakes up tomorrow, alone and empty like you deserve."

One can only hope that's the case.

"Goodbye, Ms. Belle."

And then I close the door on the best thing that's ever came into my life.

CHAPTER THIRTY-THREE

Halle

Three months later...

"My producer, Maddox, is a small dick-gina."

Remington arches a brow, taking a long pull from a beer he isn't supposed to have. "I'm almost afraid to ask what a dick-gina is. I'm assuming it's something similar to a man-gina?"

I nod, swinging my legs back and forth against the washing machine, where I'm sitting with Remington while we wait on our laundry.

In California.

Where. We. Freaking. Live.

Granted, it's not as upscale as Clyde's, and the rat that comes out at night is a little scary, but it's a step in the right direction. At least for me. For Remington, I'm not so sure.

I was distraught when I called him from Vance's three months ago, snotting and crying into the phone while I tried giving him directions. I don't even know where he got the car, though it didn't matter.

I would have hitched a ride in a manure truck if it meant getting away from Vance faster.

I still can't wrap my head around all the hurtful things he said.

He was a ginormous asshole.

But he was in pain, I knew that. I tried being patient, taking his nasty remarks until I couldn't. I didn't deserve for him to shit all over me just because he was hurting. I know you tend to take out your anger on the people who you feel like won't leave you, but Vance was purposely being cruel.

He wanted me to leave.

So, I gave him what he requested.

Solitude.

Maybe this was how it was all supposed to work out? Maybe God didn't put us together so we could heal one another fully. Maybe we were only supposed to heal *parts* of each other.

Vance gave me refined scars and a clean slate to pursue my acting career like I had always dreamed.

I gave Vance a different memory of the operating room, one where he could accept Logan's death and move past the trauma.

Now, the rest is up to us.

I couldn't heal Vance's guilt from the death of his friend, and he couldn't give me the love I thought I wanted more than my career. He showed me that I needed to make myself happy first before I could make anyone else happy.

Which is what Remington and I are doing.

We're living off cheap takeout, temporary jobs, and skeezy motel rooms.

The experience isn't quite what we thought it would be, but at least I'm not doing it alone.

"Dick-gina is way worse than man-gina," I inform Remington, handing over a bite of the Fruit Roll-Up we're currently sharing.

"What did he do today? Shit in the director's chair again?"

Rem's not being sarcastic. Maddox really did shit in the poor man's chair. Apparently, he thought he was doing a shitty job directing, and therefore, he showed him just what he thought of his directorial debut.

I meant it when I said he was a dick-gina.

"No shit this time, but he told my costar that if she didn't rid herself of ten pounds before tomorrow, she was fired."

Remington's legs stop swinging in rhythm with mine. "Has he ever said that kind of shit to you?"

My little hero is such a psycho when he wants to be.

First, he threatened to kill Vance in his sleep, which I was able to deflect by packing my bags and telling him I was leaving for California. I told him Kristen found me an audition, and I had spent enough time waiting to achieve my dreams. When I looked up from throwing clothes in the bag, Rem was gone.

But not for long.

A few minutes later, with two bags slung over his shoulder, Rem offered me a shrug and said California sounded cool. I tried telling him to stay. I still didn't know his family situation or why he lived at Clyde's and worked construction, but he assured me that he had nothing better to do, and I wasn't his mom.

So, that was that.

We bought two bus tickets to Cali, where I ended up getting the part I auditioned for with Maddox—a doctor, of all characters.

"Calm your nerves," I tell Remington, as he shoots me a glare and taps out a cigarette. "Maddox hasn't said anything nasty to me."

Yet.

It's only a matter of time. Maddox's favorite pastime is to harass his crew and make them cry. Unlike Vance, he doesn't give a shit if he's hit with a lawsuit.

Vance.

Not a day goes by that I don't think of him.

Some days, I get angry, thinking of the last thing he said to me, and other days, I think about our time in his house, doing naked stretching until we just full-out mauled each other on his Italian rug.

I wonder if he's had it cleaned since we had so many romps on it.

Part of me hopes he hasn't, and there's a certain scent lingering to remind him that what we had wasn't just a doctor-patient relationship.

What we had was real.

But until Vance can accept the truth, we have nothing to discuss.

Taking a long drag, Remington nudges me in the side. "Why do you want to work for Maddox anyway? Can't you get another acting gig?"

If it were only that simple. "I hate working for Maddox, but if I want to continue to work in show business, then I need the experience." I sigh. "And right now, Maddox is the only one willing to take a chance on a newbie."

"Fuck him."

Remington can sometimes be a man of few words, except when it comes to threats.

"Right?" I take a swig of Remington's beer as he eyes me warily. "What? Why are you looking at me like that?"

He takes another puff. "Promise you won't be mad?"

It's the first time he's sounded like a teenager.

"Cross my heart." I even make the motion to solidify the promise.

"I just see the way you come home every day."

"How do I come home?" Where is he going with this?

"You come home..." He swallows nervously. "Lifeless."

I swear my eyebrows jump to my hairline. "Lifeless?"

"Maybe lifeless was too harsh a word, more like, your spark is gone. It doesn't seem like you're happy out here, Hal."

"I'm happy," I lie before amending, "it'll get better. I just need to get through this movie with Maddox, the dick-gina, and then things will start looking up."

Remington, wiser than his age, doesn't miss a beat. "And what if the next producer screams at you, too? Or tells you that you need to lose twenty pounds to be worthy of his movie?"

"I see where you're going with this, Rem, but not every producer in show business is a giant asshole."

Sighing, he rakes his hand through his hair and adds, "I know you cry at night. You think I'm asleep, but I hear you call out his name."

I sit up straighter. "I do *not* call out for *him*."

"You do, Hal. You don't need to be embarrassed about it. You loved Vance. Those feelings won't disappear overnight."

"You sound like you have experience with such feelings."

Remington shrugs. "I suppose. Still doesn't change the fact that you do it. Regularly."

I don't know why I'm getting so defensive. It's not like Remington hasn't seen me cry over Vance. He has. A lot.

But there is something wholly personal about calling out for someone in your sleep.

"Do you miss him, Hal?"

Gah, I want to lie. I want to look at Rem and say that I miss Vance about as much as a yeast infection. But I can't. Remington might keep his secrets, but he's never lied to me, and I won't start lying to him.

My voice ends up coming out as a whisper. "All the time. And I know I shouldn't, okay? He was a royal jerk who crushed my already bruised heart. But some days… I can understand why he did it."

Remington frowns, not agreeing at all, but I keep on, "I can understand a pain so excruciating you would do anything to get away from the constant ache."

Rem opens his mouth, likely about to argue, but I hold up a finger. "I can, Rem. I've been where Vance is."

"And where is Vance, Hal? Not here, that's for sure. He's over in Bloomfield, making millions by fucking the vulnerable patients who need his help."

So, Rem is still a little pissed at Vance. That's okay. We both have our ways of dealing.

"You know that's not what happened between Vance and me."

He grabs the beer from my hand and tips it back. "According to him, that was exactly how it went down between you."

"Vance lied; he didn't mean what he said."

Remington scoffs, tossing the now empty beer bottle into the trash. "Sure, he did."

I'm not here to convince Remington of Vance's feelings for me because Remington doesn't believe in anything when it comes to love.

Someone left scars on him that I may never uncover.

I take Remington's hand in mine and squeeze. "It doesn't matter. We're here, away from Vance and the Potter brothers."

He sighs. "But you're not happy. You miss them."

I shrug. "So, maybe I do. It doesn't change the circumstances. Vance made his choice, and I made mine."

"Yeah." He laughs. "With Maddox, a bigger asshole than Vance could ever be."

"Maddox is temporary."

At least, I hope.

Remington is right, though. I do find myself in my trailer, wondering if acting is really where I'm supposed to be. I think of Vance's patient, Charlotte's daughter, often. I wonder if she ever got the surgery and was able to wear the prom dress of her dreams.

These are the things I miss the most, being in California.

Other than Vance, of course.

But I still find myself worrying if Astor is overbooking his appointments and forgetting to file his charts. Apparently, he hasn't hired another secretary since I left. But he makes sure to keep me up to date with the comings and goings of the office. Never much about Vance, though. Which is probably for the best. Knowing Vance is thriving and happy would only make my uncertainty about acting worse.

I look at Remington, his brown eyes full of concern. "Are *you* happy here, Rem?"

Moving here was my idea, but he's the one who gave up his life to come with me.

"I already told you, I had nothing better to do."

"That doesn't answer my question, though."

Sometimes I wonder if Rem has ever been happy. Occasionally, he'll laugh, and it sounds genuine, but more often than not, it's like he just goes through the motions, both of us functioning on autopilot.

Pulling his hand away, he makes this disgusted sound. "I'm happy if you're happy."

"Well, I'm still deciding."

Happiness isn't a dress you can just put on.

It takes time and hard work.

But, I'll get there.

Eventually.

CHAPTER THIRTY-FOUR

Vance

"Since we last spoke, your case settled, and your patient, Ms. Belle, has been in California."

My therapist, Dr. Johnson, is the last person I want to see right now, but after sleeping through a meeting, Astor demanded I come for a session. Honestly, I could give two shits about Astor's demands, but I haven't slept well in weeks.

I'm exhausted, grouchy, and per Astor, a real pain in the ass.

So, here I am, attempting to fix whatever is plaguing me.

"That's correct."

I try relaxing on the sofa that, I'm sure, makes most patients more comfortable. But not me. All I can think about is how the blue fabric is the same color as Halle's eyes.

"And you're back in the operating room full time now?"

I nod. "Yes, daily."

Every single time I walk into the room full of steel and straps, I think of Halle's naked body stretched out in front of me. So vulnerable, so trusting. I've had to jerk off before surgery just so I don't get a semi walking in.

"And how does operating again make you feel?"

Like something is missing.

"Fine, I guess." I shrug. I don't want to tell Dr. Johnson my issues with hard-ons in the OR. I doubt either of us would feel comfortable. I don't pay him to make me feel like a horny teenager by discussing the fact that I'm unable to control my urges regarding a certain woman.

"You guess?" He arches a brow. "How have you been sleeping?"

And this is where I really need answers. "Not well."

"Have you changed your routine lately?"

Yes, I'm not sleeping next to a naked woman who drives me batshit crazy with her defiance and sweet laughter.

"No."

"Wasn't Ms. Belle staying with you up until she left for California?"

"Yes."

"Do you think that could be factoring into your restlessness? Maybe you had unknowingly established a routine with her?"

"It was a temporary arrangement between us. She needed me to help her through recovery."

Dr. Johnson is braver than I gave him credit for. "Did she really, Dr. Potter?" He gives me this look that clearly indicates he knows I'm lying. No, I didn't *need* to help Halle recover from surgery, but I wanted to. And I'll take that information to the grave.

I exhale and adjust my tie for no other reason than so I don't storm out of here. "Yes, she had no family here and no one to change her dressings."

He nods and scribbles something on his notepad. "And how does her absence at the office feel?"

Like a big fucking absence. "I fired Serena last week, so it feels a little understaffed as we speak."

It's been a bad day—okay, maybe a bad couple of weeks.

Serena tried consoling me with hateful comments about Halle for the last time. I snapped. But Dr. Johnson doesn't need to know that.

"Have you interviewed other employees yet?"

"No, Ms. Belle was Astor's employee."

"But Serena was yours. Are you overworking yourself, Vance?"

"No. I'm just…" I rake my hands through my hair. Fuck it. "I'm lost."

Damn, that felt good to say. "For a year I lived with the stress of Logan's death and Calista's lawsuit. And then Halle threw herself into the mix. Now, all of those people are out of my life, and I don't know what to do with the emptiness."

"Have you talked to Calista since the settlement?"

I shake my head. "I doubt she ever wants to speak to me again."

"How do you know if you haven't spoken to her?"

Seriously, this guy gets paid to say the dumbest shit. "Would you want to talk to me if I killed your wife, Dr. Johnson?"

He leans forward. "I think I would like the opportunity to decide if I wanted to forgive you or not."

There's that word again, forgive.

Is it possible Calista could forgive me? I know things will never be the same between us, but…

"I think you owe yourself the chance to make amends with Calista, Dr. Potter."

"And what if she doesn't forgive me?"

"Then you'll have to forgive yourself. Either way, Vance, you have to move on. Forgiving yourself is the first step."

"I thought I had when I performed Halle's surgery," I admit.

"Being able to overcome the trauma and memory of the last time you were in the operating room is one thing, Vance. Forgiveness is another." Dr. Johnson lets out a long sigh. "Something is still keeping you in the past—from allowing you to move forward. And I think you know what that is."

Forgiveness.

Fucking forgiveness.

My watch beeps, and I'm quick to spring up. "Time's up. I'll see you next week."

Unlike me, Dr. Johnson is slow to stand, leveling me with a serious look before extending his hand for me to shake. "Move forward, Vance. Logan would want you to be happy."

Would Logan really want me to move forward and be happy? Would I, if the roles were reversed?

I think so.

I would find no joy in seeing my friend suffer. As a surgeon, Logan understood the risks we take every time we enter the operating room. Something could always go wrong; we're human after all. We make mistakes.

The last thing I wanted was for my childhood friend to lose his life by my orders.

But I can't change the past.

I can only mold my future with the pieces I have left.

Texting a number I haven't used in a year, I send a message I pray she answers.

Hanning's Cemetery 6:00

I didn't elaborate. Calista will either show or she won't. Either way, I know what I need to do.

Let the forgiving begin.

The cemetery where Logan is buried is this patch of land with rolling hills and open space behind a small, white church. It's nothing fancy, but Logan wasn't all that fancy, either. He would have thought a mausoleum was too pretentious for his body to rest for all eternity.

He would have been proud of his wife, who chose a spot on top of a hill, looking into the sunset, with a joint tombstone with her name on the other side, waiting to join his.

Dr. Johnson would find it interesting that I don't hate the thought of having my name next to the person I love—knowing that, even after death, we'll still lie next to one another. But what's more, is the name that flashes in my head is the one I pushed away, sending her to California in tears.

Dr. Johnson was right about one thing. I did have a routine with Halle. I still have a routine, technically. She's just not at Clyde's when I drive by in the morning, slowing down as I pass by. On her office desk, her pen still lies there exactly as she left it. And every evening, when I go home, I stretch before bed, leaving her side untouched.

Despite all of the same routines, I don't sleep. I'm emptier now than I was before Halle came into my life. It's frankly concerning, and I'm certain if Dr. Johnson or my brothers knew about my habits, they would have me assessed at a hospital.

Halle would understand, though.

She's always had a way of seeing through my bullshit, pulling out the pieces I wanted to keep hidden. And now… no one challenges me. Once again, I can come and go as I please, keeping the demons on a long leash. They didn't go away with Halle and the lawsuit. Like the pain, they linger, waiting for me to figure out how to manage this new life of mine, full of regret and disappointment.

"Dr. Potter," comes a soft voice at my side, where I'm sitting at the foot of Logan's grave.

I turn and lock eyes with Calista. "Is that who I am to you now? Dr. Potter?"

Tears are already gathered in her eyes. Two weeks ago, I gave Richard the directive to settle the case with Calista by offering her a lump sum settlement. It came with the conditions that I would not admit liability or give up my license or practice in any way.

Richard nearly had an aneurysm, since he clearly thought we could have won at trial, without any sort of settlement. But I still cared about Calista, no matter how awful she's been during this lawsuit. She's still family, and if a settlement helped her move on, then I wanted to try. Granted, I know money can't heal grief, but giving Calista some sort of win against me could push her in the right direction.

Both of us need to move on. Getting the lawsuit behind us was a start.

And according to Dr. Johnson, forgiveness is the next step.

"I—" Calista starts then stops, her chin quivering as her gaze roams back to Logan's headstone.

"He would have preferred a black headstone, you know?" Calista's head whips back to me, and I force out a grin. "Don't act so scandalized. You know it's true. He would have wanted to look like a badass." I wave a hand at the white granite. "This white is purely your style."

It takes a minute of her just staring at me, shocked, before she starts chuckling. "You're still an asshole."

At least it's a step up from a killer.

"You're right, Dr.—" She pauses, swallowing hard. "—Vance." Her voice lowers as she repeats my name. "You're right. He would have hated the color, but like the home we built, he got to pick the land, and I got to pick the house. I thought it was fair since this would be our last home together."

She chokes on the last bit and sobs.

I just react, pulling her into my arms. She comes easily, and I hold her tightly, like Logan would want. "I'm so sorry, Cal. So fucking sorry."

Her fists beat weakly against my chest. "I miss him so much, Vance. I can't eat. Can't sleep."

Her words hit me straight in the heart. "I miss him, too," I say softly, rocking us back and forth until she relaxes in my arms, gripping my shirt and burying her face into my chest.

"He would hate what I did to you." She snorts out a pained sound. "But I couldn't do anything but cry…"

Unfortunately, I understand what she means. "You needed a focus—something to get you through the day." A distraction from the pain.

"Yes, but I shouldn't have made that focus you." She tries to pull away, but I don't let her.

"We all deal with grief in different ways," I assure her. Though I would rather she have not attacked my credentials and practice, but I get it.

"You were our family," she agrees, pulling back and wiping away her tears. "And I blamed you. I knew Logan would have disagreed, but

I just couldn't stand to go home... to see his toothbrush... his leftovers in the fridge. It was more than I could handle. I just wanted you to feel the pain of losing everything you loved."

"Calista," I sigh, rubbing soothing circles on her back. "I had an immeasurable amount of pain. Logan was like a brother to me. I may not have experienced his loss the same way you did, but trust me, the pain was there." Really fucking there.

Calista pulls back to look me in the eyes. "I know, and I'm so sorry that I couldn't see anything but my own pain. I know you loved Logan."

"I love you, too, you know?" I swipe away a rogue tear and she laughs.

"I sure fucked that up, huh?"

"No, you didn't. I still love you, Cal—I just hope you get a bad bout of diarrhea occasionally."

A true laugh bursts out of her as she smacks my chest. "Shut up."

The air feels lighter, even though nothing has really changed between us. Deep down, I've always continued to love Calista, and I think she's felt the same. But our grief was crippling, taking away the good memories we had and covering them in darkness so we felt alone and estranged.

The words, *will you forgive me*, are right there on my tongue, just waiting to be asked.

But I hold them back.

I've allowed enough things to control my life. I don't need Calista's forgiveness to move on. Sure, I might want it, but me healing only requires forgiving myself. Asking anyone else to do it for me will only lead to disappointment.

And I'm done with that.

"I told my attorney I wanted to give the money back," Calista blurts out. "If Logan were alive, he would have divorced me for suing you in the first place."

He would have, but I don't tell her that. We're trying to make progress here.

"But he said that was between me and you. So..." She takes my hand, bowing her head. "I'd very much like your approval in opening a scholarship fund in Logan's honor for underprivileged kids who want to attend med school."

Something flutters in my chest. "I think Logan would like that very much."

"But what about you?"

I think about how much progress Calista and I have made in a matter of minutes. "I think I'd like that very much."

We might not have forgiven each other, and maybe we never will, but one thing is for sure, we are making progress.

We are moving on.

CHAPTER THIRTY-FIVE

Vance

I paid Clyde—who was a real person and not just a name of a shitty motel.

It was the first time I've ever paid for a phone number.

And after today, it better be the last.

Me: Tell me where you are.

Moody Teenager: A chapel. Hal insisted on making a man out of me.

Okay, I take it back. I'll likely need to buy another phone number when Halle changes hers after I kill Remington.

Me: I'm not in the mood.

Moody Teenager: Halle says you're never in the mood. Quite a shame really. She deserves someone younger with more stamina.

For fuck's sake. Will she really miss him? Maybe I'll just pay him off instead of killing him? I think Brazil sounds like a nice place for a teenager to roam and impregnate the locals.

Me: The address, Remington.

Moody Teenager: What are you, like fifty?

The longer I entertain his bullshit, the longer I sit in this car, just off the tarmac, in California. But, I need to know where they are without asking Halle. For all I know, she'll refuse to speak with me since I've given her nothing but radio silence these past few months while I handled my shit.

Me: I'm thirty-five, not fifty. Now, where the fuck are you?

It takes a little longer for him to respond this time, and I hope that means he's actually typing out an address and not some bullshit quip again.

Moody Teenager: Starlight Motel on 98th. You better hurry, we're packing for the airport… then your sweet southern belle will be all mine.

Normally, I'd never let some toddler threaten me, but it's been too fucking long since I've seen my girl. With Dr. Johnson's help, I'm finally to the point that I can deal with conflict without backsliding into the land of assholism.

It hasn't been easy.

This forgiving yourself shit is hard.

Halle was right, it's not something you can just say and expect it to hold. Forgiving myself is a choice. On bad days. On good days. I still make a choice, telling myself I am forgiven, and I am worthy of a life of happiness. (Dr. Johnson's words, not mine, but they work all the same.)

Me: You wouldn't know a southern belle if she poked you in the ass. Don't move. I'm coming.

I bark out the address to my driver and continue to drum my fingers against the window until my phone dings again.

Moody Teenager: What if she doesn't want to see you?

Me: Too fucking bad.

Moody Teenager: Bout time. Don't make me regret not killing you.

I don't even know how to respond to that, so I don't. I just close my eyes and pray it's not too late to grovel.

Clyde's would be considered a four-star hotel in comparison to this shithole.

"I can't believe you let her live here." Like a bad movie, Remington is in a plastic chair outside the motel door with a cigarette hanging from his mouth.

"Aww. I'm sorry it's not up to your standards, Dr. Pussy. Let me see if I can find a fuck for you to ease your stay." He grins, taking a hit off his cigarette and blows the smoke in my face. "Oh, that's right. You're not fucking staying."

I kick the legs of his piece of shit chair and send him scrambling for balance. "You're right, I'm not staying. I'm taking Halle and getting her out of this armpit." I look at the door Remington is blocking. "She in there?"

"Maybe."

Maybe I'm going to use his body to break down the door.

"She's in the shower."

I don't give him time to say more, knocking the little prick out of my way, charging through the door, and locking it behind me before he can further get in my way.

"You bastard!" Remington pounds on the door, and it makes the asshole in me smile. I appreciate him looking after my girl, but she's not his.

Halle Belle has always belonged to me.

Moving into the room, I try not to focus on the holes in the walls and the cigarette burns in the curtains. Instead, I follow the steam into the bathroom, where the door is cracked and only a shower curtain separates me from my sweet Georgia peach.

"Remington?" she calls out, probably having heard all the pounding going on outside. "Is that you?"

Pushing the door open fully, I walk into the bathroom and stand at the plastic curtain not hiding the curves of her body. There's so much I need to say, so much I need to make right between us, but all I can do is stand there with my tongue stuck to the roof of my mouth.

"Rem—" The curtain is yanked to the side, and Halle's flushed face appears. "Vance?"

I blink in rapid succession. I don't know what I was expecting, but seeing her again—whole, with the same brilliant blue eyes and southern accent—has rendered me mute.

"What are you doing here, Vance?"

What am I fucking doing here?

Halle might be living in a shithole, but she seems to like them. She looks healthy and happy with dipshit out front. She's moved on, and I'm here, trying to drag her back.

Without a word, I shake my head and try for an apologetic smile, which apparently concerns Halle.

"Vance, are you okay? Talk to me."

After all that I've done to her, she's still consoling me. No matter how many times I repeat that I deserve happiness, I will never be worthy of this woman. She deserves so much more than I can offer her.

"I—" I take a step back. I need to get out of here before I fuck her life up even more.

But then she gets out of the shower. Her naked body is stunning as I take in her healed scars, flat stomach, and... worried eyes.

She puts her hands on my shoulders and—fuck it.

I drop to my knees, wrapping my arms around her legs. "Forgive me," I beg, bowing my head and fighting back the emotion clogging my throat. "Forgive me, Peach. I've been such a bastard to you."

Halle's fingers thread through my hair. "Bastard is putting it lightly." She chuckles, and it's the sweetest sound I've heard in months.

"That's true," I agree, "I said some awful things you didn't deserve to hear."

"No, I didn't, Vance, but you said them anyway, because you wanted to hurt me."

"No." I try shaking my head, but Halle holds it still with her hands. "I wanted to hurt myself, and you kept pulling me out of this dark place where it was easier to deal with the pain."

I can feel my shirt getting wetter as the water drips from Halle's body.

"And are you happier in that dark place?" She lifts my head and forces me to meet her gaze. Seeing her now, with all her goodness, I realize what an epic fool I've been.

"No, Peach, I'm not happy there. I never was."

I can see the tears well in her eyes, but she doesn't let them fall. My beautifully strong girl… She was always braver than me. "Why are you here, Vance? What do you want from me?"

Everything.

Whatever you'll give me.

But I'll start with, "Forgiveness." I press a kiss to her bare stomach. "I took your advice, I forgave myself, but I can't move forward without…" *You.* "…your forgiveness. I did wrong by you, Halle, and I'm not naïve enough to expect that you'll offer me a second chance, but I'm hoping you'll grace me with forgiveness. I don't want to be another man who takes even a minute away from your happiness. You deserve a future full of possibilities and good memories. Don't let my behavior be the dark spot that takes away from your beautiful soul."

For a moment, the only noise is the shower running. Halle doesn't speak, and my chest burns in response. She doesn't forgive me, and like I knew would happen, disappointment settles in.

But this isn't about me.

This is about Halle and her future.

I might want to throw her over my shoulder and drag her back to Bloomfield, but it would be a selfish decision. So, even if I'd rather drown myself in Oscar's fishbowl than live without Halle in my life, I will, because I love her.

I want to see her happy, even if it's without me.

With one last press of my lips to her body, I stand, slipping my jacket off and draping it over her shoulders as tears streak down her face. "I needed you to know that I am so very sorry."

There's no need to tell her that I love her. I fucked up the right to love her when I basically told her she was nothing but a patient to me. This is my punishment. Leaving her with a teenager, who needs his ass kicked just as hard as mine. "I promise this is the last time I'll bother you."

I allow myself one last look at her. One last memory before I let her go and move on. "Good—"

"I forgive you!" Her words are garbled with her sobs, but I'm pretty sure that's what she says. "I *fucking* love you, Vance! Does that make you happy?"

Okay, so that definitely cleared things up.

I close my eyes and inhale. I've waited to hear those words, but the lightness didn't come like it had with Calista. "No, Peach. I'm never happy seeing you cry." But the love thing I can definitely live with.

She snorts out a bitter laugh. "Why can't you just say what you mean? Why do always have to be drunk to say what you really feel?"

"You don't want to know how I really feel."

Suddenly, we're chest to chest, each of us panting against the other.

"Yeah, I think I do, Dr. Potter." Her eye twitches as her hands ball at her sides. "Don't be shy now."

She tries shoving me, and I grab her wrists. "Okay, fine." Fuck it. "I love you, goddammit!" I yank her to me. "I don't want to know you're happy here with fuckboy. I want to sling you over my shoulder and drag you from this shithole and back to Bloomfield, where you belong. In. My. Bed." I drop one of her hands and grip her chin. "You were mine the minute you insulted me."

Her lips twitch as she fights off a smile. "And you were going to what? Bow out like a gentleman since I didn't answer you?"

There it is, that bullshit that pushes my buttons, inciting a level of excitement than can only be worked out between the sheets. "I was trying to do the right thing." My lips hover over hers.

"Never take no for an answer, Dr. Potter. I thought you would have learned that by now."

I smash my lips against hers, my hands roaming around to her backside as I soak up every inch of her that I've missed.

Finally, I come up for air with reality settling in. "Hollywood could use another plastic surgeon, don't you think?"

Pressing a finger to my lips, she shakes her head. "No, I think you're right where you belong in Bloomfield."

"But…"

How am I supposed to see her and run my practice in Texas at the same time?

"I'm coming home, Dr. Potter."

I rear back. "To Bloomfield?"

She nods. "I might have gotten fired for punching my producer in the face."

"Oh, shit," I lift her in my arms in this ridiculously small bathroom, "you are vicious. Does that mean we can get out of here before we're eaten up by bedbugs?"

She slaps my chest and presses her lips to mine. "On one condition."

EPILOGUE

Vance
Two years later…

“I won't say I'll miss you.”

“Vance!”

Halle smacks my arm, and I grin at the little prick in front of me, his arms stacked with boxes.

Remington can barely see over the top of the cardboard when he stops in the center of the room and unceremoniously drops them. “Fuck you, Potter. No one is missing your hateful ass, either. I feel sorry for Hal having to stomach you all alone.”

I cast a wicked grin at Halle, who has decided to fret over the packed dishes that Remington likely broke by dropping the shit on the floor. “Oh, she'll stomach me a lot more now that you're out of the house.”

“You're disgusting,” he notes, grinning, not offended in the least. This sort of talk, we're used to. It's how we've managed not to kill each other all this time.

“And you're a pain in my ass. Happy college life, kid.” I pull out the package in my jacket pocket—a box of condoms—and toss it to him. "Don't knock up anyone. Babies are expensive, and so are you. I can only afford one."

Halle frowns at me then at Remington. "I'll never understand your relationship. You would think you two hate each other."

Maybe at first, we did.

Like me, Remington is a sucker when it comes to persuasion by a certain blonde. When it came time to leave California, Halle refused to leave Remington at the squatty motel. He tried arguing, but when Halle started crying, he got in the car like a good little boy.

Remington, she learned, was seventeen, and while I thought he could take care of himself just fine, Halle felt like he'd done so much for her that it was only right that she pay it forward until he could afford a place on his own.

It was supposed to be a temporary situation.

Two years and a GED later, temporary finally came to pass. After spending those past two years at Potter's Plastics, serving as my assistant—Halle refused to leave Astor and work for me, claiming she would kill me before lunch—Remington has decided that surgeons get plenty of pussy, and he wants in on this scam. His words, not mine.

Either way, my unexpectedly great assistant is starting college. He decided on Halle's alma mater in Georgia, which annoyed me for all of about four seconds until he said, "Do you really want Hal coming to check on me every weekend, or would you prefer keeping her locked away in your bedroom for forty-eight hours?"

I couldn't help him pack fast enough.

"Do you want me to help you unpack?" Halle's voice pulls me back to the situation at hand—getting rid of the nosy teenager.

"No. He wants us to leave so we have time to squeeze in a celebratory fucking before we have to get back to Oscar."

The fish, who has a tank that spans an entire wall of the house, is the same fish I hired someone to feed while we made this trip to Georgia.

"Vance! What is up with you today?" Halle seems quite offended with my behavior, but little does she know, the kid and I had an agreement. It's time to see it through. The longer she plays Mommy Dearest, the longer I'm delayed in fulfilling my end of the bargain.

"Naw. I can manage. It's just a few boxes anyway."

That's because I—well, my assistant—had the furniture shipped and assembled prior to our arrival. Other than his dishes and clothes, Remington should be all set. Which is what I need right now since I spent the past three hours on a jet, not able to distract Halle like I normally would. Instead, we played video games, which left me with a raging case of blue balls.

So, time for my assistant to spread his wings and make my girl happy, knowing he's getting the second chance he deserves.

"Are you sure? Vance and I can stay and—"

I place my hand over her mouth. "He'll be fine. I, however, won't be if we have to stay here much longer."

I'm already getting hives being in shitty dorms again. What's more, I had to endure Halle's stiff posture and silent tears as we drove through Frat Row, the location that changed her life irrevocably.

"Fine." She sighs, flashing Remington a regretful look. "You sure you're gonna be okay?"

Pulling her into his arms, he tucks her head under his chin, silently threatening me with a look as he says, "I'll be fine. Call me later, kay?"

Because he won't believe me when I tell him she's fine.

"Okay. I'm gonna miss you, neighbor." Halle squeezes him, and I know that no matter how far apart we are from Remington, we'll always be family. The past two years together solidified a bond I hadn't even realized I wanted.

The kid might have given me shit eight hours a day as my assistant, but he was a good kid. He was genuine with patients and a real pain in my ass when I missed my therapy appointments. Which, Halle insisted he try, too. We were both at her mercy but came out better men because of her.

"I'll miss you, too, Hal." He rubs her back and mouths, *I'll fucking kill you if you hurt her,* over the top of her head.

Which, I'm all too happy to return with my own silent warning, *"I'll cut off your credit cards and repo your car. Test me, little boy."*

His car is a '67 Chevy Impala we gifted him for his eighteenth birthday. It's his most coveted possession, and I won't hesitate to bring it back to Texas if he fucks up his GPA.

He nods and then grins, kissing the top of Halle's head and stepping back. "Take care of the boss. He's going to be a real asshole come Monday, when he's dealing with the new guy."

I groan. He's not wrong. Since he's leaving, I had to hire someone from a temp agency. I'm certain I'll fire Nate, the "new guy," as Remington calls him. So far, he's asked me eighteen billion questions and even came into the bathroom to tell me I was late for my therapy appointment last week. I'm positive Halle and Rem put him up to it.

Halle turns back to me and laughs. "I'll make sure and keep him alive."

I'm not sure if she's talking about me or the new guy at this point. Either way, it doesn't matter. It's time to finish this. "See ya later, kid." I pull Halle to me, so she can't try giving out one last hug, and pat Remington on the shoulder. "Don't fuck this up."

The kid might be annoying, but he has potential and will make a damn fine surgeon one day.

Inevitably, Halle goes in for another round of hugs, but I finally manage to get us into the car and down the block. "This isn't the way to the airport," she notices.

"We're not going to the airport yet."

She swallows, noting the houses as we top the hill. "Vance…" Her tone is wary. "Why are we on Frat Row?"

"I need to do one last thing before we go home."

This might be the worst idea I've ever had, but Halle once told me that sometimes, in order to move on, we need to create good memories atop of the bad ones.

I can't guarantee this will help her like it did me, but I'm hoping it won't make things worse. We pull up to the three-story colonial, with peeling paint and broken siding, and park.

Getting out, I walk to the passenger side and open her door, squatting down so I'm eye level. "Will you trust me?" I hold out my hand, waiting for her to start crying and tell me to fuck off.

But she doesn't.

Instead, she nods and places her hand in mine. With all the gentleness I have, I ease her from the car and walk us around to the center of the driveway and kneel.

Halle's eyes widen as tears start to fall.

"This place holds a memory—one that I can never erase." I swallow hard, not wanting to fuck this up. "But I can mold this memory into something different. This very driveway took the old Halle from a man who never deserved her."

Halle chokes on a sob and squeezes my hand.

"But this place also gave me that same beautiful soul..."

I pull the black box from my coat pocket and open it. "I'm completely selfish for taking you away from someone more deserving, but I'm too in love with you to care."

Taking the ring from the box, I hover it over Halle's finger. "I want the last memory of this place to be you promising me your future. I want it all, Ms. Belle. From weekend visits to see Remington to fucking right here on this very driveway. I want the opportunity to change every memory you have of this place into something beautiful."

I slide the ring on her finger. She really has no option of saying no here. "Because, Peach, I've never seen someone more beautiful on the inside and out. Marry me. Marry me, and let me make you happy. I promise, I can."

Sinking to her knees, Halle grabs my face. "On one condition."

"Anything," I promise.

She grins, pressing a soft kiss to my lips. "Admit that you and Remington were the ones who bashed in Caleb's car and set it on fire last year."

Technically, it wasn't just me and Remington. Astor found his address—I didn't ask how, and Duke suggested we all take a trip to Georgia to help Halle's parents move into their new home.

"I have no idea what you're talking about."

I can't help it Caleb was easy to find. He shouldn't have stayed in his hometown.

"You're lying, Dr. Potter," she threads her fingers through my hair, tilting my head back, "and it's never been sexier."

"Does that mean you'll marry me?"

I could be reading the whole situation wrong here.

"I'll marry you, Dr. Potter." She kisses me hard, taking us to the ground, where we make new memories out of the scars that brought us together in the first place.

"Seriously," Remington interrupts us. "I thought you said it was a G-rated proposal."

I don't know how I missed the sound of his loud ass Impala coming down the street. "It was until Halle decided to make you a little brother out here on the driveway."

We were just kissing. Rest assured, no one received a free show, but that doesn't mean I don't like to see Remington gag at the mention of a little brother.

He helps Halle from the ground and kisses her cheek. "Congratulations, Ms. Potter." He hands over his lighter. "Do you want to do the honors, or would you like me to?"

Halle's head volleys back and forth between us. "What are you talking about?"

Remington shrugs. "We thought a cake was too cliche to celebrate, so Vance bought the house instead."

"What!" She flips around and pins me with a serious look. "Did you really buy this house?"

Maybe this wasn't such a good idea after all? "Would it make you feel better if I lied and said I put it on layaway first?"

Remington laughs, and she snatches the lighter from his hand. "And y'all want me to burn it down as way of celebrating?"

I shrug and pull the deed to the home from my pocket. "You can, or we can remodel it and turn it into an outpatient facility for students with substance abuse problems. Your choice, Ms. Potter."

Halle looks at me, then at Remington, her eyes gleaming with unshed tears. "Oh, Vance."

Yeah, I probably should have led with the house.

"I love you." She throws herself into my arms. "So, so much."

My soon-to-be wife, the beautiful soul that just wouldn't take no for an answer, might not have accomplished her dream of being on the big screen, but the impact she makes every day at Potter's Plastics and the impact she'll have here, at this facility, has and will continue to change lives.

And that's exactly the happily ever after she deserves.

Did you love the Potter family? Want to see more broody heroes like Vance? Check out **Commander** and fall in love with the grumpy men of the McCallister Jameson Foundation.

Subscribe to my VIP listing to be notified of all future release dates.

Love *The Potter*? Want to read more from me?
All of my books are standalone and are free in Kindle Unlimited.

OTHER BOOKS BY
KRISTY MARIE

21 Rumors
*A Romantic Comedy Series- All novels are standalone and feature
different couples with crossover characters*

IOU
Subscriber Wars
The Closer

The Commander Legacies
*A Second-Generation Contemporary Series- All novels are standalone
and feature different couples with crossover characters*

Rebellious

Commander in Briefs
*A Contemporary Series- All novels are standalone and feature different
couples with crossover characters*

Pitcher
Gorgeous
Drifter
Interpreter

In the Hands of the Potters
*A Contemporary Series- All novels are standalone and feature different
couples with crossover characters*

The Potter

Come hang out in my Facebook reader group, Kristy's Commanders, for exclusive content and sneak peeks of my newest releases.

Sign up to receive updates on all my new releases and participate in juicy giveaways.

Check out my website and purchase signed copies of your favorite paperback.

Follow me!

Amazon
www.amazon.com/author/mariekristy

BookBub
www.bookbub.com/authors/kristy-marie

Instagram
www.instagram.com/authorkristymarie

Facebook
www.facebook.com/authorkristymarie

Twitter
www.twitter.com/authorkristym

Goodreads
www.goodreads.com/author/show/17166029.Kristy_Marie

ACKNOWLEDGMENTS

See, what had happened was… LOL!

Oh, man. I waited until the final hour to get this book done. Literally, my editors were cleaning up my mess hours before this book had to be finalized.

I take no credit in the fact you're getting to read this story right now.

I merely had an idea, stopped writing Fenn's book (I know, I should be shot), developed this series, and put it into motion—all at the last minute.

Then came the plague.

The kids brought it home and shared the love like the sweet, little angels they are.

Needless to say, my good intentions, last-minute book, and notorious procrastination came around and bit me in the ass. Hard.

These women—these very patient, very amazing women, made this book happen. I could not have done it without them.

Jaime, one day, I'll actually give you a deadline I can meet. Until then, please just continue to love me for who I am—a crazy, unorganized nut who loves you. I can never thank you enough for always coming through for me—usually at the last minute. Okay, always at the last minute. Thank you for making me shine!

Sarah P., is it too early to ask when I can see you again? Right, I'll wait a few days. But seriously, thank you for reading this book so many times and making sure I met my deadline. You're a superhero!

Rebecca, I think it's safe to say you're stuck with me. I'm sorry, I know it's not ideal, but I love you—and your edits—to give you up. #imselfish. Thank you for dealing with my mess and never making me feel bad about it. I <3 U.

Autumn, should I just send flowers for this book? I kinda put you through hell with all the drama and scheduling. Oh, right, you're used to it. Still, do you like tulips? A thank you just won't suffice.

Jessica, hello? Do you remember me? I am your friend, who can't answer messages timely or chat anymore. I blame it on the kids. But I still love you and very much appreciate you holding the fort down while I rocked in a corner.

Sarah S., CHOO FREAKING CHOO! I think we should invest in more trains, huh? It's time we realized our destinies are tied to the #hotmessexpress. We'll be okay, though. We have each other forever and ever. #clingly #youmakemepretty

Melody, Keri, Aundi, and Ri, ummm... I kinda suck, but I'm glad you guys are used to it. Thank you for always riding the crazy wave with me. You keep me going when I want to quit.

Amy, Catherine, and Rebecca, I think it's safe to say the words in this book came from peer pressure. Thank you for always cheering me on and bringing out my competitive side. I love you guys!

Letitia of RBA designs, unfortunately for you, I love you. Therefore, you are forever stuck trying to come up with better ways to avoid me. You blew this cover out of the water, though, boo. Bravo, my cover whisperer.

Stacy of Champagne Designs, I thank God every day that you're so flexible with my insanity. You truly bring my stories to life with your beautiful designs.

To the most remarkable reader group ever established: Kristy's Commanders. You guys inspire me every day and keep me motivated to always give you the best storylines I can dream up. YOU. ARE. THE. REAL. DEAL.

And last, but certainly not least, to you, who's reading this page. You are the reason I do this. Thank you for reading my words and purchasing this book. I owe you everything.